W9-DFY-175

U.S. EDITION

PRIMARY MATHEMATICS 5B

TEXTBOOK

Education Resource Center
University of Delaware
Newark, DE 19716-2940

T 57050

SingaporeMath.com Inc

Marshall Cavendish
Education

Original edition published under the title Primary Mathematics 5B

© 1984 Curriculum Planning & Development Division

Ministry of Education, Singapore

Published by Times Media Private Limited

This American Edition

© 2003 Times Media Private Limited

© 2003 Marshall Cavendish International (Singapore) Private Limited

Published by Marshall Cavendish Education

A member of Times Publishing Limited

Times Centre, 1 New Industrial Road, Singapore 536196

Customer Service Hotline: (65) 6411 0820

E-mail: fps@sg.marshallcavendish.com

Website: www.marshallcavendish.com/education/sg

Distributed by

SingaporeMath.com Inc

404 Beavercreek Road #225

Oregon City, OR 97045

U.S.A.

Website: http://www.singaporemath.com

First published 2003

Second impression 2003

Third impression 2004

Fourth impression 2005

Fifth impression 2005

Sixth impression 2006

Reprinted 2006, 2007

All rights reserved. No part of this publication may be
reproduced, stored in a retrieval system or transmitted,
in any form or by any means, electronic, mechanical,
photocopying, recording or otherwise, without the prior
permission of the copyright owner.

ISBN 978-981-01-8511-4

Printed in Singapore by Times Graphics Pte Ltd

ACKNOWLEDGEMENTS

Our special thanks to Richard Askey, Professor of Mathematics (University of Wisconsin,
Madison), Yoram Sagher, Professor of Mathematics (University of Illinois, Chicago), and Madge
Goldman, President (Gabriella and Paul Rosenbaum Foundation), for their indispensable
advice and suggestions in the production of Primary Mathematics (U.S. Edition).

PREFACE

Primary Mathematics (U.S. Edition) comprises textbooks and workbooks. The main feature of this package is the use of the **Concrete** ➡ **Pictorial** ➡ **Abstract** approach. The students are provided with the necessary learning experiences beginning with the concrete and pictorial stages, followed by the abstract stage to enable them to learn mathematics meaningfully. This package encourages active thinking processes, communication of mathematical ideas and problem solving.

The textbook comprises 9 units. Each unit is divided into parts: ❶, ❷, . . . Each part starts with a meaningful situation for communication and is followed by specific learning tasks numbered 1, 2, . . . The textbook is accompanied by a workbook. The sign [Workbook Exercise ⟩ is used to link the textbook to the workbook exercises.

Practice exercises are designed to provide the students with further practice after they have done the relevant workbook exercises. Review exercises are provided for cumulative reviews of concepts and skills. All the practice exercises and review exercises are optional exercises.

The color patch ■ is used to invite active participation from the students and to facilitate oral discussion. The students are advised not to write on the color patches.

CONTENTS

1 Decimals

1 Approximation and Estimation

The weight of the watermelon is 4.728 kg.

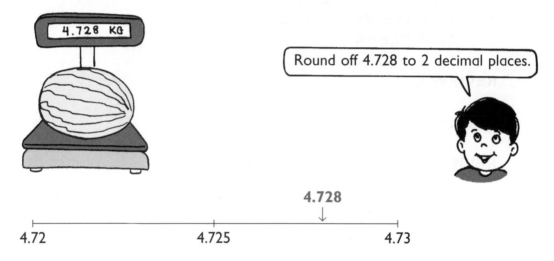

Round off 4.728 to 2 decimal places.

4.728 is more than halfway between 4.72 and 4.73. It is rounded off to 4.73. We write:

4.728 ≈ 4.73

The weight of the watermelon is **about** 4.73 kg.

1.

3.148 is ■ when rounded off to 2 decimal places.
3.141 is ■ when rounded off to 2 decimal places.
3.145 is ■ when rounded off to 2 decimal places.

> To round off a number to 2 decimal places, we look at the digit in the third decimal place. If it is 5 or greater than 5, we round up; if it is less than 5, we round down.

2. Round off each of the following to 2 decimal places.
   (a) 5.168   (b) 8.044   (c) 10.805   (d) 23.718

Workbook Exercise 1

3. Find the value of 24.65 ÷ 8 correct to 2 decimal places.

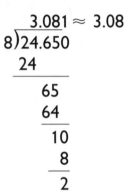

$$\frac{3.081}{8)24.650} \approx 3.08$$

$$\underline{24}$$

$$65$$
$$\underline{64}$$
$$10$$
$$\underline{8}$$
$$2$$

Divide to 3 decimal places. Then round off the answer to 2 decimal places.

4. Find the value of each of the following correct to 2 decimal places.
   (a) 0.77 ÷ 9   (b) 62.7 ÷ 7   (c) 9.65 ÷ 8
   (d) 41.51 ÷ 6   (e) 27.69 ÷ 4   (f) 20.93 ÷ 3

Workbook Exercise 2

5. Express $4\frac{2}{3}$ as a decimal correct to 2 decimal places.

$$\frac{2}{3} \approx \blacksquare$$

$$4\frac{2}{3} \approx \blacksquare$$

$$\frac{0.666}{3)2.000} \approx 0.67$$

$$\underline{1\ 8}$$
$$20$$
$$\underline{18}$$
$$20$$
$$\underline{18}$$
$$2$$

6. Express each fraction as a decimal correct to 2 decimal places.
   (a) $\frac{3}{7}$ (b) $\frac{5}{8}$ (c) $\frac{2}{9}$ (d) $\frac{1}{6}$

   (e) $5\frac{7}{9}$ (f) $1\frac{1}{3}$ (g) $4\frac{5}{7}$ (h) $8\frac{3}{8}$

Workbook Exercise 3

2 Multiplication by Tens, Hundreds or Thousands

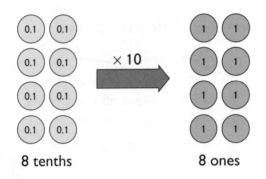

8 tenths → 8 ones

$$0.8 \times 10 = 8$$

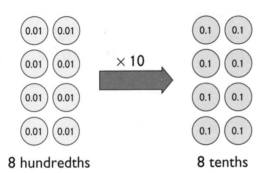

8 hundredths → 8 tenths

$$0.08 \times 10 = 0.8$$

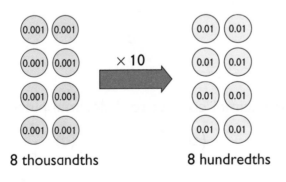

8 thousandths → 8 hundredths

$$0.008 \times 10 = 0.08$$

1. Multiply.
   (a) 0.6×10 (b) 0.8×10 (c) 0.9×10
   (d) 0.02×10 (e) 0.04×10 (f) 0.03×10
   (g) 0.005×10 (h) 0.006×10 (i) 0.007×10

2. Multiply 3.42 by 10.

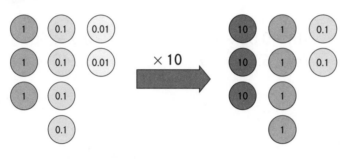

$3.42 \times 10 = 34.2$

3. Multiply 0.035 by 10.

Tens	Ones	Tenths	Hundredths	Thousandths
			× 10 3	× 10 5
		3	5	

$0.035 \times 10 = 0.35$

When a decimal is multiplied by 10, we move the decimal point 1 place to the right.

0.035

4. Multiply.
   (a) 0.12×10 (b) 0.068×10 (c) 0.345×10
   (d) 2.05×10 (e) 3.21×10 (f) 1.439×10
   (g) 7.5×10 (h) 10.4×10 (i) 11.8×10

5. Multiply 0.53 by 40.

    $0.53 \times 40 = 2.12 \times 10$

    $\qquad = $

    $0.53 \times 4 = 2.12$

6. Multiply.
    (a) 0.006×30 (b) 0.08×40 (c) 0.9×50
    (d) 0.32×20 (e) 6.81×70 (f) 3.248×60

    Workbook Exercise 4

7. Multiply 0.007×100.

    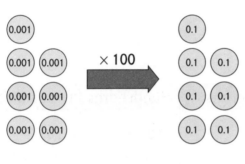

    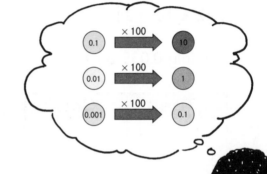

    $0.007 \times 100 = $ ■

8. Multiply 4.23 by 100.

Hundreds	Tens	Ones	Tenths	Hundredths
	× 100	4 × 100	2 × 100	3
4	2	3		

$4.23 \times 100 = 423$

When a decimal is multiplied by 100, we move the decimal point 2 places to the right.

4.23

10

9. Multiply 0.006 by 1000.

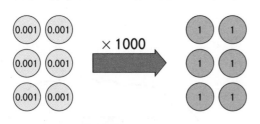

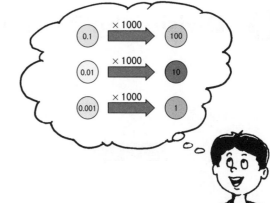

$0.006 \times 1000 = \blacksquare$

10. Multiply 0.054 by 1000.

Tens	Ones	Tenths	Hundredths	Thousandths
		× 1000	5	×1000 4
5 ←	4 ←			

$0.054 \times 1000 = 54$

When a decimal is multiplied by 1000, we move the decimal point 3 places to the right.

11. Multiply.
    (a) 0.003×100 (b) 3.2×100 (c) 1.325×100
    (d) 0.09×1000 (e) 3.62×1000 (f) 13.4×1000

Workbook Exercise 5

12. Multiply 4.203 by 200.
    $4.203 \times 200 = 8.406 \times 100$
    $\qquad\qquad\quad = \blacksquare$

$4.203 \times 2 = 8.406$

13. Multiply 4.203 by 2000.
    $4.203 \times 2000 = 8.406 \times 1000$
    $\qquad\qquad\qquad = \blacksquare$

14. Multiply.
    (a) 0.008×300 (b) 0.12×600 (c) 1.54×400
    (d) 0.03×5000 (e) 0.25×6000 (f) 5.12×4000

Workbook Exercise 6

③ Division by Tens, Hundreds or Thousands

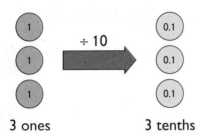

3 ones → 3 tenths

3 ÷ 10 = 0.3

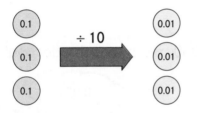

3 tenths → 3 hundredths

0.3 ÷ 10 = 0.03

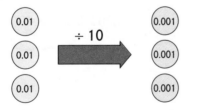

3 hundredths → 3 thousandths

0.03 ÷ 10 = 0.003

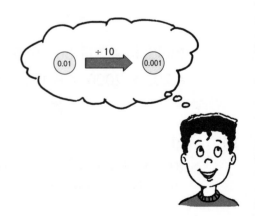

1. Divide.
   (a) 8 ÷ 10
   (b) 0.8 ÷ 10
   (c) 0.08 ÷ 10
   (d) 2 ÷ 10
   (e) 0.2 ÷ 10
   (f) 0.02 ÷ 10
   (g) 6 ÷ 10
   (h) 0.6 ÷ 10
   (i) 0.06 ÷ 10

2. Divide 0.46 by 10.

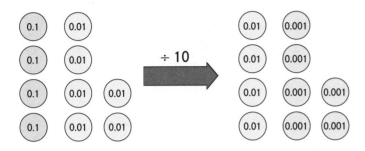

   0.46 ÷ 10 = 0.046

3. Divide 5.3 by 10.

Tens	Ones	Tenths	Hundredths	Thousandths
	5	÷ 10 3	÷ 10	
		5	3	

   5.3 ÷ 10 = 0.53

   When a decimal is divided by 10, we move the decimal point 1 place to the left.

   5.3

4. Divide.
   (a) 0.23 ÷ 10
   (b) 0.45 ÷ 10
   (c) 0.12 ÷ 10
   (d) 2.5 ÷ 10
   (e) 6.8 ÷ 10
   (f) 5.3 ÷ 10
   (g) 12 ÷ 10
   (h) 39 ÷ 10
   (i) 103 ÷ 10

5. Divide 4.2 by 60.

$4.2 \div 60 = 0.7 \div 10$

$\quad = $

 4.2 ÷ 6 = 0.7

6. Divide.
   (a) $8 \div 40$ (b) $16 \div 80$ (c) $63 \div 90$
   (d) $4.8 \div 60$ (e) $0.51 \div 30$ (f) $3.44 \div 80$

Workbook Exercise 7

7. Divide 4 by 100.

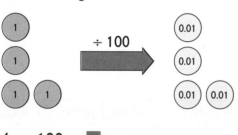

$4 \div 100 = $ ▇

8. Divide 52.8 by 100.

Tens	Ones	Tenths	Hundredths	Thousandths
5	÷ 100 2	÷ 100 8	÷ 100	
		→ 5	→ 2	→ 8

$52.8 \div 100 = 0.528$

When a decimal is divided by 100, we move the decimal point 2 places to the left.

52.8

14

9. Divide 5 by 1000.

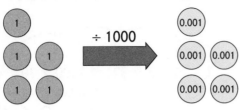 

$5 \div 1000 = $ ▪

10. Divide 62 by 1000.

Tens	Ones	Tenths	Hundredths	Thousandths
6	2		÷ 1000	
		÷ 1000	6	2

$62 \div 1000 = 0.062$

When a decimal is divided by 1000, we move the decimal point 3 places to the left.

062.0

11. Divide.
(a) $8 \div 100$ (b) $90 \div 100$ (c) $1.5 \div 100$
(d) $4 \div 1000$ (e) $200 \div 1000$ (f) $324 \div 1000$

Workbook Exercise 8

12. Divide 46 by 200.

$46 \div 200 = 23 \div 100 = $ ▪

$46 \div 2 = 23$

13. Divide 46 by 2000.

$46 \div 2000 = 23 \div 1000 = $ ▪

14. Divide.
(a) $0.8 \div 200$ (b) $1.6 \div 400$ (c) $4.8 \div 300$
(d) $12 \div 6000$ (e) $65 \div 5000$ (f) $714 \div 7000$

Workbook Exercise 9

4 Multiplication by a 2-digit Whole Number

Multiply 2187 by 32.

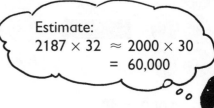

Estimate:
2187 × 32 ≈ 2000 × 30
= 60,000

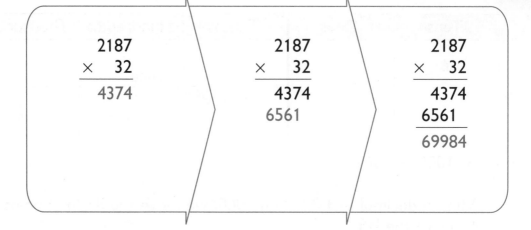

```
  2187          2187          2187
×   32        ×   32        ×   32
  4374          4374          4374
                6561          6561
                             69984
```

Multiply 21.87 by 32.

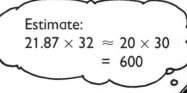

Estimate:
21.87 × 32 ≈ 20 × 30
= 600

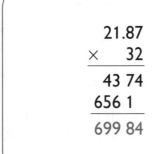

```
  21.87              21.87
×    32            ×    32
  43 74             43 74
  656 1             656 1
  699 84            699.84
```

16

1. Estimate the value of
   (a) 3267×28

   $3267 \times 28 \approx 3000 \times 30 = $ ■

   (b) 326.7×28

   $326.7 \times 28 \approx 300 \times 30 = $ ■

   (c) 32.67×28

   $32.67 \times 28 \approx 30 \times 30 = $ ■

Workbook Exercise 10

2. (a) Estimate the value of 0.23×59.

   $0.23 \times 59 \approx 0.2 \times 60 = 12$

   (b) Find the value of 0.23×59.

$$
\begin{array}{r}
0.23 \\
\times 59 \\
\hline
2\ 07 \\
11\ 5 \\
\hline
13\ 57 \\
\end{array}
\qquad
\begin{array}{r}
0.23 \\
\times 59 \\
\hline
2\ 07 \\
11\ 5 \\
\hline
13.57 \\
\end{array}
$$

3. Multiply.
   (a) 0.78×43 (b) 0.53×23 (c) 37×4.9
   (d) 23.7×26 (e) 40.6×45 (f) 18×132.4
   (g) 3.58×43 (h) 15.09×26 (i) 72×1.57

Workbook Exercise 11

5 Conversion of Measurements

The table shows the heights of 3 boys in meters. Express the heights in centimeters.

Name	Height
Sam	1.4 m
Ryan	1.26 m
Matthew	1.32 m

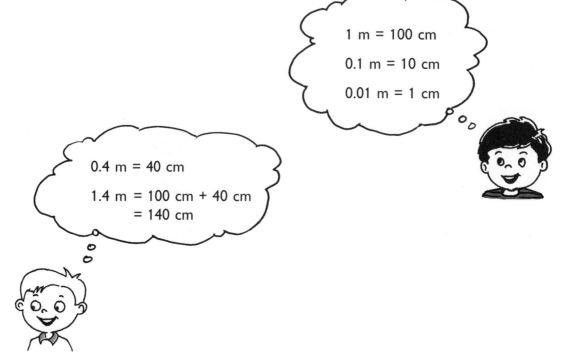

1 m = 100 cm

0.1 m = 10 cm

0.01 m = 1 cm

0.4 m = 40 cm

1.4 m = 100 cm + 40 cm
     = 140 cm

Sam's height is 140 cm.

Ryan's height is ▮ cm.

Matthew's height is ▮ cm.

1. (a) Express 0.75 m in centimeters.

   0.75 m = 0.75 × 100 cm

   = ■ cm

   (b) Express 3.75 m in centimeters.

   3.75 m = 3.75 × 100 cm

   = ■ cm

   (c) Express 0.5 ft in inches.
   0.5 ft = 0.5 × 12 in.
   = ■ in.

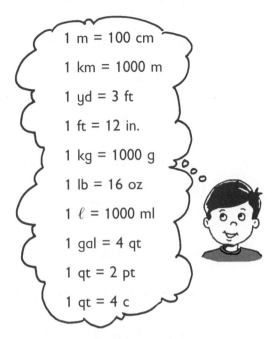

1 m = 100 cm

1 km = 1000 m

1 yd = 3 ft

1 ft = 12 in.

1 kg = 1000 g

1 lb = 16 oz

1 ℓ = 1000 ml

1 gal = 4 qt

1 qt = 2 pt

1 qt = 4 c

2. (a) Express 2.8 kg in grams.

   2.8 kg = 2.8 × 1000 g

   = ■ g

   (b) Express 6.25 lb in ounces.

   6.25 lb = 6.25 × 16 oz

   = ■ oz

3. Find the equivalent measures.
   (a) 0.6 m = ■ cm
   (b) 0.49 ℓ = ■ ml
   (c) 0.615 km = ■ m
   (d) 0.3 kg = ■ g
   (e) 1.85 kg = ■ g
   (f) 4.2 ℓ = ■ ml
   (g) 2.5 m = ■ cm
   (h) 1.05 km = ■ m
   (i) 2.75 qt = ■ c
   (j) 3.5 lb = ■ oz
   (k) 3.25 ft = ■ in.
   (l) 0.5 gal = ■ qt

4. Express 4.2 ℓ in liters and milliliters.

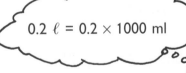

0.2 ℓ = 0.2 × 1000 ml

   4.2 ℓ = 4 ℓ ■ ml

5. Find the equivalent measures.
   (a) 4.6 m = ■ m ■ cm
   (b) 7.4 km = ■ km ■ m
   (c) 1.2 kg = ■ kg ■ g
   (d) 5.9 ℓ = ■ ℓ ■ ml
   (e) 3.45 km = ■ km ■ m
   (f) 2.06 m = ■ m ■ cm
   (g) 4.005 ℓ = ■ ℓ ■ ml
   (h) 6.432 kg = ■ kg ■ g
   (i) 4.25 lb = ■ lb ■ oz
   (j) 7.5 ft = ■ ft ■ in.

Workbook Exercise 12

6. Express 145 ml in liters.

$$145 \text{ ml} = \frac{145}{1000} \ell$$

$$= \blacksquare \ \ell$$

145.0

7. Find the equivalent measures.
   (a) 350 m = ■ km
   (b) 420 ml = ■ ℓ
   (c) 625 g = ■ kg
   (d) 30 cm = ■ m

8. (a) Use a tape measure to find your friend's height in meters and centimeters.
   (b) Express the height in meters.

500 g = 0.5 kg

9. Express 3 kg 500 g in kilograms.

   3 kg 500 g = 3 kg + 0.5 kg

   $= \blacksquare$ kg

10. Find the equivalent measures.
    (a) 4 m 35 cm = ■ m
    (b) 5 km 90 m = ■ km
    (c) 2 ℓ 800 ml = ■ ℓ
    (d) 4 kg 75 g = ■ kg
    (e) 3 ft 9 in. = ■ ft
    (f) 3 qt 2 c = ■ qt

Workbook Exercise 13

11. Express 3080 g in kilograms.

    Method 1:

    3080 g = 3 kg 80 g

    $= \blacksquare$ kg

    Method 2:

    $$3080 \text{ g} = \frac{3080}{1000} \text{ kg}$$

    $= \blacksquare$ kg

3080.0

12. Find the equivalent measures.
    (a) 4070 m = ■ km
    (b) 2380 ml = ■ ℓ
    (c) 5200 g = ■ kg
    (d) 605 cm = ■ m
    (e) 51 in. = ■ ft
    (f) 88 oz = ■ lb

Workbook Exercise 14

PRACTICE 1A

1. Round off each of the following to 2 decimal places.
   (a) 0.119　　(b) 7.508　　(c) 40.082　　(d) 81.143
   (e) 0.725　　(f) 3.123　　(g) 59.005　　(h) 18.607

2. Round off each of the following to 2 decimal places.
   (a) 6.265 km　(b) 4.083 kg　(c) 0.189 ℓ　(d) 20.245 ℓ

3. Express each fraction as a decimal correct to 2 decimal places.
   (a) $\dfrac{1}{8}$　　(b) $\dfrac{4}{7}$　　(c) $2\dfrac{5}{9}$　　(d) $5\dfrac{2}{3}$

Find the value of each of the following:

	(a)	(b)	(c)
4.	10×5.7	100×1.508	7.25×1000
5.	30×0.002	400×3.29	6.8×3000
6.	84×0.13	56×2.07	1.29×29
7.	$39 \div 10$	$34.2 \div 100$	$9 \div 1000$
8.	$99 \div 30$	$648 \div 600$	$60 \div 2000$

Find the equivalent measures.

9. (a) 0.285 ℓ = ■ ml　　(b) 0.75 gal = ■ qt
   (c) 0.085 km = ■ m　　(d) 0.25 ft = ■ in.
   (e) 0.706 kg = ■ g　　(f) 0.5 lb = ■ oz

10. (a) 670 ml = ■ ℓ　　(b) 12 oz = ■ lb
    (c) 105 m = ■ km　　(d) 3 c = ■ qt
    (e) 69 g = ■ kg　　(f) 6 in. = ■ ft

11. (a) 20.08 km = ■ km ■ m　　(b) 3.75 qt = ■ qt ■ c
    (c) 16.5 ℓ = ■ ℓ ■ ml　　(d) 18.5 ft = ■ ft ■ in.
    (e) 2.08 kg = ■ kg ■ g　　(f) 4.75 lb = ■ lb ■ oz

12. (a) 9 m 60 cm = ■ m　　(b) 6 gal 3 qt = ■ qt
    (c) 4 ℓ 705 ml = ■ ℓ　　(d) 2 lb 5 oz = ■ oz
    (e) 25 km 6 m = ■ km　　(f) 3 ft 7 in. = ■ in.

13. Juliana is 1.64 m tall. Her sister is 6 cm shorter. Find her sister's height in meters.

14. Rachel had 3.54 kg of flour. She used 250 g to make cookies and 1.25 kg to bake cakes. How many kilograms of flour did she have left?

REVIEW A

1. What is the value of the digit 5 in each of the following?
    (a) 10.275   (b) 58,026   (c) 36.254

2. Write each of the following as a decimal.
    (a) 50 + 0.8 + 0.006   (b) 7 + 0.03 + 0.001
    (c) $45 + \dfrac{3}{10} + \dfrac{8}{1000}$ (d) $8 + \dfrac{9}{1000}$

3. (a) What number is 0.01 more than 12.6?
    (b) What number is 0.1 less than 10?

4. Arrange the numbers in increasing order.
    (a) 31,238,   31,832,   31,823,   31,328
    (b) $4\dfrac{1}{6}$, $\dfrac{9}{2}$, $4\dfrac{2}{5}$, $4\dfrac{3}{10}$
    (c) 4.98,   4.089,   498,   4809
    (d) $2\dfrac{1}{2}$,   2.05, $2\dfrac{3}{5}$,   2.51

5. Divide. Give each answer as a decimal.
    (a) 42 ÷ 5   (b) 23 ÷ 4   (c) 15 ÷ 8

6. Express each fraction as a decimal correct to 2 decimal places.
    (a) $\dfrac{3}{7}$ (b) $\dfrac{2}{9}$ (c) $3\dfrac{5}{6}$

7. Express each decimal as a fraction in its simplest form.
    (a) 0.062   (b) 2.36   (c) 6.308

8. Find the value of each of the following.
    (a) 3000 × 400   (b) 6.04 × 3000   (c) 3.25 × 62
    (d) 48,000 ÷ 2000   (e) 48.9 ÷ 100   (f) 6.5 ÷ 2

9. Find the value of each of the following:
    (a) 23 × (34 − 25)   (b) 7 × 8 + 48 ÷ 3
    (c) (45 − 31) × 4 + 12   (d) (28 + 9) × (12 − 7)

10. Find the value of each of the following in its simplest form.
    (a) $\dfrac{2}{3} \times 45$ (b) $\dfrac{35}{12} \times \dfrac{18}{7}$ (c) $\dfrac{7}{9} \div 5$

11. Find the missing number in each ■.
    (a) 2.06 kg = ■ kg ■ g   (b) 1.73 km = ■ m
    (c) 50 cm = ■ m   (d) 2008 ml = ■ ℓ
    (e) $\frac{1}{2}$ h = ■ min   (f) $2\frac{1}{6}$ years = ■ months
    (g) $5\frac{3}{4}$ km = ■ m   (h) $8\frac{3}{8}$ ℓ = ■ ℓ ■ ml

12. Josh bought a motorcycle for which he paid a deposit of $210 and 10 monthly installments of $31.25 each. Find the cost of the motorcycle.

13. Mrs. Garcia bought 2.5 kg of sugar. She used 325 g of it to make cookies and 1.45 kg to make cakes. How much sugar did she have left? Give the answer in kilograms.

14. Mrs. Cohen bought 15 m of string. She used 2.5 m to tie a package. Then she cut the remainder into 6 equal pieces. Find the length of each piece. Give the answer in meters correct to 1 decimal place.

15. Susan bought 10 apples and 8 pears. The apples cost $0.35 each. A pear cost twice as much as an apple. How much did she pay altogether?

16. Mrs. Smith used $\frac{3}{8}$ of a bag of flour to bake cakes and $\frac{1}{5}$ of the remainder to bake biscuits. What fraction of the flour did she use altogether?

17. Henry bought 1 liter of fruit juice. He kept $\frac{1}{4}$ liter of it in a bottle and poured the remainder equally into 6 cups. How much fruit juice was there in each cup? Give the answer in liters.

18. Mr. Venezia sold $\frac{1}{3}$ of his eggs in the morning and $\frac{1}{4}$ in the afternoon. He had 320 eggs left. How many eggs did he have at first?

19. The ratio of the number of female members to the number of male members in a club is 3 : 5. If there are 48 female members, how many members are there altogether?

20. The area of a rectangle is 300 m². If the length of the rectangle is 20 m, find its width and perimeter.

21. Find the perimeter and area of the figure. (All lines meet at right angles.)

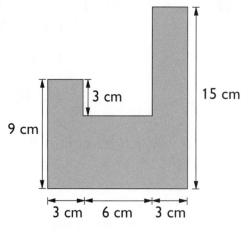

22. Find the area of the shaded part of the rectangle.

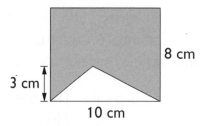

23. Find the area of the shaded figure.

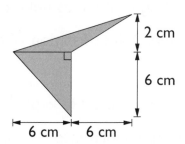

24. In each of the following figures, not drawn to scale, find $\angle x$.
(a) ABC is a straight line.   (b)

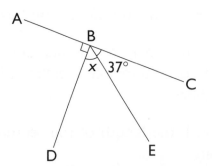
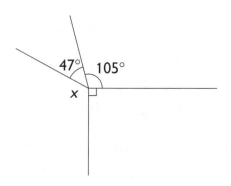

2 Percentage

1 Percent

There are 100 seats in a theater.
55 seats are occupied.

55% of the seats are occupied.

55% means **55 out of 100**.

We read 55% as **55 percent**.

55% is another way of writing $\frac{55}{100}$ or 0.55.

1. 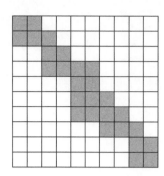 The whole is divided into 100 equal parts.
27 parts are shaded.
What **percentage** of the whole is shaded?

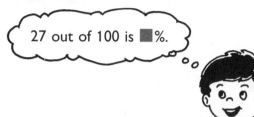
27 out of 100 is ■%.

2. What percentage of the whole is shaded?

(a)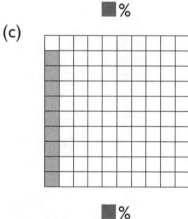

■%

(b)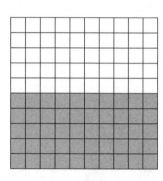

■%

(c)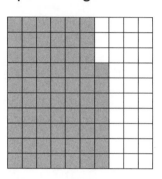

■%

(d)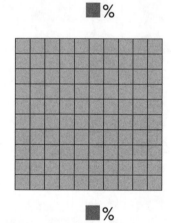

■%

3. Write each of the following as a percentage.
   (a) 33 out of 100   (b) 20 out of 100   (c) 5 out of 100

4. Express each fraction as a percentage.

$\frac{3}{10} = \frac{30}{100}$

(a) $\frac{23}{100}$ (b) $\frac{45}{100}$ (c) $\frac{36}{100}$ (d) $\frac{75}{100}$

(e) $\frac{40}{100}$ (f) $\frac{70}{100}$ (g) $\frac{3}{10}$ (h) $\frac{5}{10}$

Workbook Exercise 15

5. Express 0.35 as a percentage.

$$0.35 = \frac{35}{100}$$

$$= \blacksquare\%$$

6. Express each decimal as a percentage.
    (a) 0.07   (b) 0.02   (c) 0.85   (d) 0.7

7. Express 43% as a decimal.

$$43\% = \frac{43}{100}$$

$$= \blacksquare$$

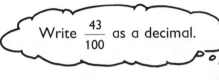
Write $\frac{43}{100}$ as a decimal.

8. Express each percentage as a decimal.
    (a) 28%   (b) 88%   (c) 30%   (d) 5%

Workbook Exercise 16

9. [flower grid image]

40% of the flowers are roses. What fraction of the flowers are roses?

$$40\% = \frac{40}{100}$$

$$= \blacksquare$$

Write $\frac{40}{100}$ in its simplest form.

$\blacksquare$ of the flowers are roses.

10. Express each percentage as a fraction in its simplest form.
     (a) 10%   (b) 80%   (c) 25%   (d) 75%
     (e) 5%   (f) 8%   (g) 4%   (h) 2%

Workbook Exercise 17

② Writing Fractions as Percentages

Mr. Goldberg has painted $\frac{3}{4}$ of a wall. What percentage of the wall has he painted?

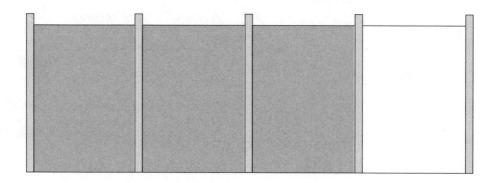

Method 1:

$$\frac{3}{4} = \frac{75}{100}$$

$$= \blacksquare\%$$

Method 2:

$$\frac{3}{4} = \frac{3}{4} \times 100\%$$

$$= \blacksquare\%$$

1 whole is 100%.

$\frac{3}{4}$ is $\frac{3}{4}$ of 100%.

He has painted $\blacksquare$% of the wall.

1. Express each fraction as a percentage.

   (a)

    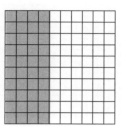

   $$\frac{2}{5} = \frac{4}{10} = \blacksquare\%$$

   (b)

    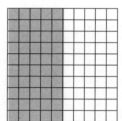

   $$\frac{1}{2} = \frac{5}{10} = \blacksquare\%$$

2. Express 7 out of 25 as a percentage.

   Method 1:

   $$\frac{7}{25} = \frac{28}{100} = \blacksquare\%$$

   Method 2:

   $$\frac{7}{25} = \frac{7}{25} \times 100\% = \blacksquare\%$$

3. Limei has 20 apples. 14 of them are red apples. What percentage of the apples are red apples?

   $$\frac{14}{20} = \blacksquare\%$$

   14 out of 20

   $\blacksquare$% of the apples are red apples.

4. Express each fraction as a percentage.

   (a) $\frac{1}{4}$ (b) $\frac{2}{5}$ (c) $\frac{4}{5}$ (d) $\frac{9}{20}$

   (e) $\frac{13}{20}$ (f) $\frac{6}{25}$ (g) $\frac{14}{25}$ (h) $\frac{41}{50}$

   Workbook Exercise 18

5. Express 180 out of 300 as a percentage.

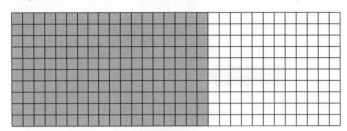

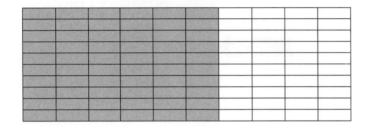

Method 1:

$$\frac{180}{300} = \frac{60}{100} = \blacksquare\%$$

Method 2:

$$\frac{180}{300} = \frac{180}{300} \times 100\% = \blacksquare\%$$

6. 200 children are at a concert. 98 of them are boys. What percentage of the children are boys?

$$\frac{98}{200} = \blacksquare\%$$

98 out of 200

$\blacksquare\%$ of the children are boys.

7. Express each fraction as a percentage.

(a) $\dfrac{8}{200}$ (b) $\dfrac{36}{200}$ (c) $\dfrac{60}{300}$ (d) $\dfrac{129}{300}$

(e) $\dfrac{40}{400}$ (f) $\dfrac{128}{400}$ (g) $\dfrac{20}{500}$ (h) $\dfrac{255}{500}$

Workbook Exercise 19

8. What percentage of each of the following bars is shaded? (Use the percentage scale to help you.)

(a)
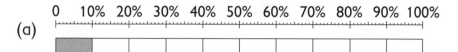

(b)

(c)

(d)
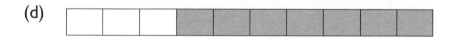

(e)

1 whole is 100%.

9. $\frac{3}{4}$ of the pies which Mrs. Goodman made were apple pies.

(a) What percentage of the pies were apple pies?

$$\frac{3}{4} = \frac{3}{4} \times 100\% = 75\%$$

■% of the pies were apple pies.

(b) What percentage of the pies were not apple pies?

$$100\% - 75\% = ■\%$$

■% of the pies were not apple pies.

10. 7 out of 25 children are boys.
(a) What percentage of the children are boys?
(b) What percentage of the children are girls?

11. Sam had $750. He spent $300 and saved the rest. What percentage of the money did he save?

Workbook Exercise 20

PRACTICE 2A

1. Express each fraction as a percentage.
    (a) $\dfrac{25}{100}$ (b) $\dfrac{5}{100}$ (c) $\dfrac{7}{10}$ (d) $\dfrac{9}{25}$

    (e) $\dfrac{3}{4}$ (f) $\dfrac{11}{20}$ (g) $\dfrac{1}{2}$ (h) $\dfrac{3}{5}$

    (i) $\dfrac{144}{300}$ (j) $\dfrac{50}{250}$ (k) $\dfrac{36}{180}$ (l) $\dfrac{8}{160}$

2. Express each decimal as a percentage.
    (a) 0.63   (b) 0.05   (c) 0.2   (d) 0.5

3. Express each percentage as a fraction in its simplest form.
    (a) 46%   (b) 5%   (c) 7%   (d) 80%

4. Express each percentage as a decimal.
    (a) 15%   (b) 41%   (c) 9%   (d) 50%

5. 15 out of 100 oranges in a box are rotten. What percentage of the oranges are rotten?

6. There are 100 marbles in a bag. 37 of them are green. The rest are red. What percentage of the marbles are red?

7. A football team won 60% of its games. What fraction of the games did the football team win?

8. If 70% of a tank is filled with water, what percentage of the tank is not filled?

9. $\dfrac{4}{5}$ of the books in a library are fiction books. What percentage of the books are fiction books?

10. There are 50 vehicles in a parking lot. 14 of them are motorcycles. What percentage of the vehicles are motorcycles?

11. Peter answered 18 out of 20 questions correctly. What percentage of the questions did he answer correctly?

12. 1500 people took part in a walkathon. 450 of them were school children. The rest were adults. What percentage of the participants were adults?

13. Tracy bought 5 kg of flour. She used 2 kg to make cookies and the rest to make pineapple tarts. What percentage of the flour did she use to make pineapple tarts?

③ Percentage of a Quantity

There were 500 people at a concert. 30% of them were children.
How many children were there at the concert?

Method 1:

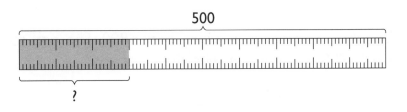

500

?

1% of $500 = \dfrac{500}{100} = 5$

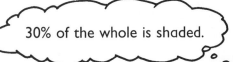
30% of the whole is shaded.

30% of $500 = 5 \times 30$

$= \blacksquare$

There were ▪ children at the concert.

Method 2:

30% of $500 = \dfrac{30}{100} \times 500$

$= \blacksquare$

$30\% = \dfrac{30}{100}$

There were ▪ children at the concert.

1. 120 students took part in a physical fitness test. 90% of them passed the test. How many students passed the test?

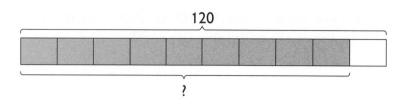

    90% of 120 = ▧

2. Lindsey bought a refrigerator which cost $800. She had to pay 3% sales tax on $800. How much was the sales tax?

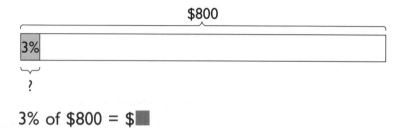

    3% of $800 = $▧

3. Find the value of
    (a) 5% of 300   (b) 8% of 200   (c) 20% of 50 kg
    (d) 25% of 40 m   (e) 45% of 70 km   (f) 75% of 400 g

    ┌─────────────────────┐
    │ Workbook Exercise 21 │
    └─────────────────────┘

4. William had $500. He spent 24% of his money on transport and 36% on food.
    (a) What percentage of his money was left?

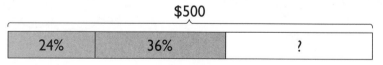

    100% − 24% − 36% = 40%

    ▧% of his money was left.

    1 whole is 100%.

(b) How much money was left?

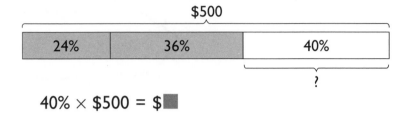

$40\% \times \$500 = \$\blacksquare$

$\$\blacksquare$ was left.

5. There were 400 members in a swimming club. 12% of the members were children. The rest were adults. How many adults were there?

Method 1:

$100\% - 12\% = 88\%$

88% of the members were adults.

$88\% \times 400 = \blacksquare$

There were $\blacksquare$ adults.

Method 2:

Number of children = $12\% \times 400 = 48$

Number of adults = $400 - 48 = \blacksquare$

Workbook Exercise 22

6. Ahmad has $2700 in a savings bank. The interest rate is 3% per year. How much money will he have in the bank after 1 year?

Find the interest for 1 year first.

Interest = 3% of $2700 = $\blacksquare$

Amount of money in the bank after 1 year

= $2700 + Interest

= $\blacksquare$

7. A man bought a refrigerator at a discount of 12%. Its usual price was $900. How much did he pay for the refrigerator?

Discount = 12% of $900

Discount = $■

Amount of money paid = $900 – Discount

= $■

Workbook Exercise 23

8. Jason's monthly salary was $1500 in May. It was increased by 8% in June. What was his salary in June?

Increase = 8% of $1500

Increase in salary = $■

Salary in June = $1500 + Increase

= $■

9. There were 400 members in a chess club last year. The membership was decreased by 5% this year. How many members are there this year?

Decrease = 5% of 400

Decrease = ■

Number of members this year = 400 – Decrease

=

Workbook Exercise 24

PRACTICE 2B

1. Find the value of each of the following:
   (a) 8% of 82   (b) 27% of $450   (c) 33% of 100
   (d) 40% of 308   (e) 75% of 148 kg   (f) 62% of 520 m

2. There are 1200 people living in a small town. 45% of them are children. How many children are there?

3. The area of a garden is 60 m². 7% of it is taken up by a pond. What is the area of the pond?

4. There were 50 words in a spelling test. Sally spelled 90% of them correctly. How many words did she spell correctly?

5. There are 20 workers in a library. 55% of them are females. How many male workers are there?

6. Tasha earns $1350 monthly. She saves 30% of the money. How much does she save each month?

7. A swimming club had 720 members last year. This year the membership increased by 5%. Find the number of members this year.

8. Mary bought a swimsuit which cost $50. In addition, she had to pay 3% sales tax. How much did she pay for the swimsuit?

9. The usual price of a camera was $190. At a sale, it was sold at a discount of 30%. What was the sale price?

10. Mrs. Meier deposited $3500 in a bank. The bank paid 3% interest per year. How much money did she have in the bank after 1 year?

11. Travis shot 15 arrows. 40% of the arrows hit the target. How many arrows did not hit the target?

12. A library has a reading club. 30% of the members of the club are boys, 40% are girls and the rest are adults. If there are 280 members, how many of them are adults?

13. There are 200 spaces in a parking lot. 10% are for vans, 75% are for cars and the rest are for motorcycles. How many spaces are for motorcycles?

3 Average

1 Average

These bags do not have the same number of oranges.

If the oranges are rearranged so that the bags have the same number of oranges, how many oranges will there be in each bag?

4 + 9 + 5 = 18

There are 18 oranges altogether.

18 ÷ 3 = 6

There will be 6 oranges in each bag.

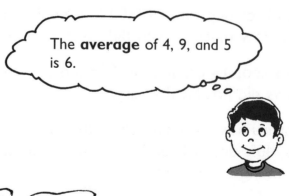

The **average** of 4, 9, and 5 is 6.

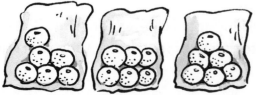

1.

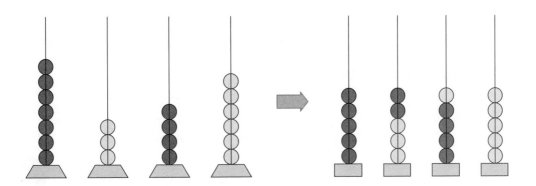

What is the average of 7, 3, 4 and 6?

$7 + 3 + 4 + 6 = 20$

The sum is 20.

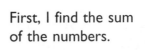

First, I find the sum of the numbers.

$20 \div 4 = $ ■

The average is ■.

2. This picture graph shows the number of fish caught by 3 boys. On the average, how many fish did each boy catch?

Ahmad	🐟 🐟 🐟 🐟 🐟
Chandran	🐟 🐟 🐟 🐟 🐟 🐟 🐟
Jinfa	🐟 🐟 🐟

$5 + 7 + 3 = 15$

The 3 boys caught 15 fish altogether.

$15 \div 3 = $ ■

On the average, each boy caught ■ fish.

39

3. Sally collected 36 stamps, Mary collected 38 stamps and Lilian collected 40 stamps.
   What was the average number of stamps each girl collected?

   Total number of stamps collected

   = 36 + 38 + 40

   = ■

To find the average number of stamps, I divide the total number of stamps by the number of girls.

   Average number of stamps collected = ■

   Workbook Exercise 25

4. The lengths of 5 strings are 1.4 m, 1.8 m, 2 m, 2.6 m and 3.2 m.
   (a) What is the total length of the 5 strings?
   (b) What is their average length?

   To find the average length, I divide the total length by the number of strings.

5. The table shows the points scored by Ron for 4 tests.
   (a) What is his total score for the 4 tests?
   (b) What is his average score?

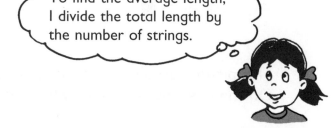

Test A	68
Test B	76
Test C	78
Test D	88

   Workbook Exercise 26

6. A taxi driver traveled a total distance of 1659 km in 7 days. Find the average distance he traveled per day.

   1659 km ÷ 7

7. Jesse's average score for 5 tests is 74.6.
   Find his total score.

8. Warner spent an average of $4.65 per day for 8 days.
   How much did he spend altogether?

$4.65 × 8

Workbook Exercise 27

9. The average weight of 3 packages is 1 kg 400 g.
   Find their total weight.

   Total weight = 1 kg 400 g × 3
   = ■ kg ■ g

   1 kg 400 g
   / \
   1 kg   400 g

10. The total weight of 4 packages is 5 kg 200 g.
    Find their average weight.

    Average weight = 5 kg 200 g ÷ 4
    = ■ kg ■ g

    5 kg 200 g
    / \
    5 kg   200 g

11. David took 15 minutes 20 seconds to cycle a distance of 2 km. On
    the average, how long did he take to cycle 1 km?

12. Peter cycled from his house to the beach which was 3 km away.
He took an average of 2 minutes 45 seconds to cycle 1 km.
How long did the journey take?

Workbook Exercises 28 & 29

13. The average height of two boys is 1.55 m.
The height of one boy is 1.62 m.
What is the height of the other boy?

First, I find the total height of the boys.

$1.55 \times 2 = 3.10$

The total height of the two boys is 3.1 m.

$3.1 - 1.62 =$ ■

The height of the other boy is ■ m.

14. The average cost of 3 books is $4.50.
The average cost of two of the books is $3.90.
Find the cost of the third book.

$\$4.50 \times 3 = \$13.50$

The total cost of the 3 books is $13.50.

$\$3.90 \times 2 = \$7.80$

The total cost of two of the books is $7.80.

$\$13.50 - \$7.80 = \$$ ■

The cost of the third book is $■.

Workbook Exercise 30

PRACTICE 3A

1. Find the average of each of the following:
   (a) 12.5, 36.2, 30.4 and 26.1
   (b) $1.35, $4.82, $3.05, $2.70 and $2.13
   (c) 3.5 kg, 3.8 kg, 4.1 kg and 5 kg
   (d) 4.6 ℓ, 6.4 ℓ, 5.8 ℓ and 3.8 ℓ
   (e) 2.62 m, 2.08 m, 3.9 m and 0.96 m
   (f) 12.2 km, 25.6 km, 9.5 km and 30.3 km
   (g) 4.81 gal, 3.52 gal, 3.59 gal and 2 gal
   (h) 9.5 in., 7.25 in., 11.9 in., 4.11 in. and 6.09 in.

2. Rowley traveled 5460 km in 3 months. What was the average distance he traveled per month?

3. A man has 6 packages. Their average weight is 18 kg. Find the total weight of the 6 packages.

4. 4 people had lunch together. They spent an average of $3.75 each. What was the total cost of the lunch?

5. On the average, Violet spent 1 hour 20 minutes a day reading storybooks.
   How much time did she spend reading storybooks in 5 days?

6. Sam used 10 ℓ 275 ml of gas in 3 days. On the average, how much gas did he use per day?

7. The average cost of 2 storybooks was $2.45. One of the books cost $2.80. Find the cost of the other book.

8. An average of 145 people visited a 4-day exhibition in the first 3 days. Another 205 people visited the exhibition on the fourth day. What is the average number of visitors per day?

4 Rate

1 Rate

A machine fills 60 bottles of syrup in 5 minutes. How many bottles of syrup can it fill in one minute?

The machine fills the same number of bottles every minute.

In 5 minutes, the machine fills 60 bottles.
In 1 minute, it fills ■ bottles.

$60 \div 5 = 12$

The machine fills the bottles at the **rate** of 12 bottles per minute. It means the machine fills 12 bottles every minute.

1. Robert is paid $20 for working 4 hours. How much is he paid per hour?

    The rate is $5 per hour.

    20 ÷ 4 = 5

    He is paid $5 per hour.

2. Water is flowing from a tap at the rate of 100 liters every 4 minutes. Find the rate of flow of water in liters per minute.

    100 ℓ in 4 min
    ■ ℓ in 1 min

    100 ÷ 4 = ■

    The rate of flow of water is ■ ℓ per minute.

    Workbook Exercise 31

3. A machine makes toy cars at the rate of 120 per minute. How many toy cars will it make in 6 minutes?

    120 toy cars in 1 min
    ■ toy cars in 6 min

    120 × 6 = ■

    It will make ■ toy cars in 6 minutes.

4. A lamp can flash 5 times per minute. At this rate, how many times can it flash in 30 minutes?

    5 times in 1 min
    ■ times in 30 min

    5 × 30 = ■

    The lamp can flash ■ times in 30 minutes.

    Workbook Exercise 32

5. Water is flowing from a tap at the rate of 25 gal per minute.
   (a) How much water can be collected from the tap in 5 minutes?

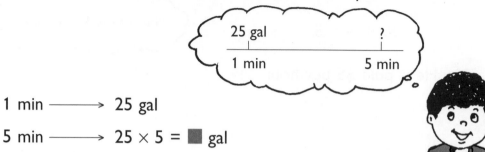

1 min ——→ 25 gal

5 min ——→ 25 × 5 = ■ gal

■ gal of water can be collected from the tap in 5 minutes.

(b) How long will it take to fill a container of capacity 100 gal?

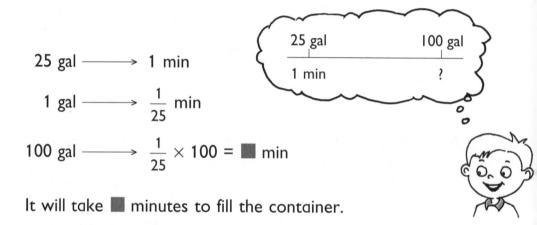

25 gal ——→ 1 min

1 gal ——→ $\frac{1}{25}$ min

100 gal ——→ $\frac{1}{25}$ × 100 = ■ min

It will take ■ minutes to fill the container.

6. Mrs. Ricci types 45 words per minute. At this rate, how long will she take to type 135 words?

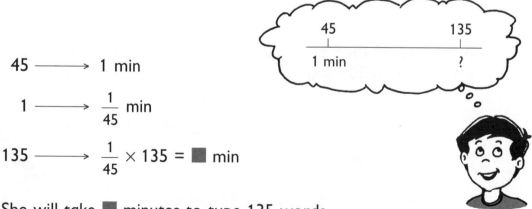

45 ——→ 1 min

1 ——→ $\frac{1}{45}$ min

135 ——→ $\frac{1}{45}$ × 135 = ■ min

She will take ■ minutes to type 135 words.

Workbook Exercise 33

7. A car can travel **96** km on 8 liters of gas.
The rate is _____ km per liter.

(a) How far can the car travel on 15 liters of gas?

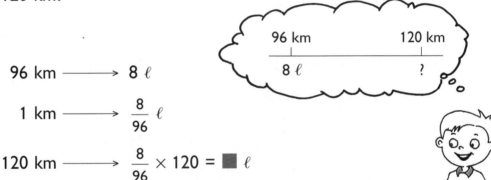

$8\ \ell \longrightarrow 96$ km

$1\ \ell \longrightarrow \dfrac{96}{8} = 12$ km

$15\ \ell \longrightarrow 12 \times 15 = \blacksquare$ km

The car can travel ■ km on 15 ℓ of gas.

(b) How much gas will be used if the car travels a distance of 120 km?

96 km $\longrightarrow 8\ \ell$

1 km $\longrightarrow \dfrac{8}{96}\ \ell$

120 km $\longrightarrow \dfrac{8}{96} \times 120 = \blacksquare\ \ell$

■ ℓ of gas will be used.

8. A photocopier can print 12 copies in 48 seconds. At this rate, how many copies can it print in 1 minute?

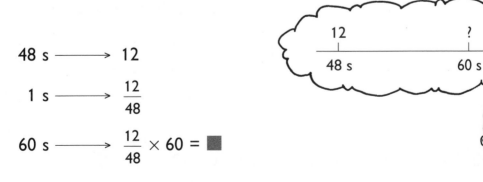

48 s $\longrightarrow 12$

1 s $\longrightarrow \dfrac{12}{48}$

60 s $\longrightarrow \dfrac{12}{48} \times 60 = \blacksquare$

It can print ■ copies in 1 minute.

Workbook Exercise 34

9. The table shows the rates of charges at a parking lot.

8:00 a.m. to 5:00 p.m.	$1 per $\frac{1}{2}$ hour
After 5:00 p.m.	$1 per hour

Mr. Karlson parked his car there from 1:30 p.m. to 7:00 p.m. How much did he have to pay?

The duration from 1:30 p.m. to 5:00 p.m. is $3\frac{1}{2}$ h.

Parking fee from 1:30 p.m. to 5:00 p.m.　= $7

Parking fee from 5:00 p.m. to 7:00 p.m.　= $2

Total parking fee = $▇

10. The workers in a factory are paid the following rates.

Weekdays	$28 per day
Saturdays and Sundays	$38 per day

Mr. Henderson worked from Friday to the following Tuesday. How much was he paid?

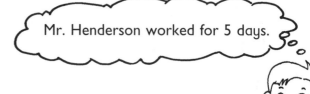

Mr. Henderson worked for 5 days.

Mr. Henderson's pay for 3 weekdays = $28 × 3 = $▇

Mr. Henderson's pay for Saturday and Sunday = $38 × 2 = $▇

Total pay = $▇

11. The table shows the postage rates for sending magazines to another state.

Weight step not over	Postage
20 g	$0.30
50 g	$0.40
100 g	$0.70
Per additional step of 100 g	$0.60

(a) Find the postage for a magazine which weighs 85 g.

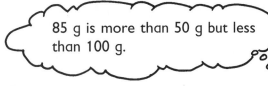

85 g is more than 50 g but less than 100 g.

Postage for 85 g = $▇

(b) Find the postage for a magazine which weighs 330 g.

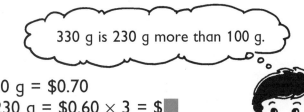

330 g is 230 g more than 100 g.

Postage for the 1st 100 g = $0.70
Postage for the next 230 g = $0.60 × 3 = $▇
Total postage = $▇

12. In a city, the rates of charges for taxi fare are as follows:

For the first km	$2.40
For every additional km	$0.40

Find the taxi fare for a trip of $5\frac{1}{2}$ km.

Fare for the 1st km = $2.40

Fare for the next $4\frac{1}{2}$ km = $0.40 × 5 = $▇

Total fare = $▇

Workbook Exercise 35

PRACTICE 4A

1. A machine can print 50 pages per minute. At this rate, how long will it take to print 2500 pages?

2. A machine takes 4 minutes to seal 16 cookie boxes. How many cookie boxes can it seal in 1 minute?

3. Maggie's heart beats at the rate of 152 times every 2 minutes. At this rate, how many times does it beat in 30 minutes?

4. A pool is filled with water at the rate of 100 gal every 5 minutes. How long will it take to fill the pool with 1000 gal of water?

5. The cost of cementing 30 m² of floor area is $810. How much will it cost to cement 55 m² of floor area?

6. A wheel covers a distance of 40 m when it makes 25 revolutions. At this rate, what distance will it cover when it makes 50 revolutions?

7. The table shows the postage rates for letters for delivery in Singapore. Find the postage for a letter which weighs
    (a) 55 g
    (b) 400 g

Weight step not over	Postage
20 g	$0.22
50 g	$0.30
100 g	$0.50
250 g	$0.80
500 g	$1.50

8. The rental rates of a ski chalet are as follows:

Weekdays	$60 per day
Saturdays and Sundays	$80 per day

    (a) Warner rented the chalet from Friday to Sunday. How much rent did he pay?

    (b) A group of friends rented 2 chalets from Wednesday to Saturday. How much did they pay altogether?

5 Graphs

1 Line Graphs

This table shows the attendance at a swimming pool for 5 months.

Month	August	September	October	November	December
Number of people	2500	3500	2000	2500	4000

The data can also be presented in a **line graph**.

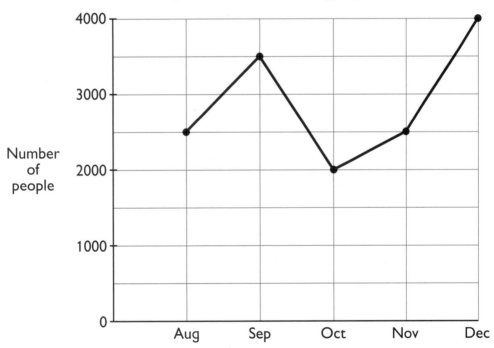

(a) There was an increase in attendance from August to September. What was the increase?

(b) There was a decrease in attendance from September to October. What was the decrease?

(c) What was the difference between the attendance in September and the attendance in December?

1. The line graph shows the number of people in a supermarket by the hour from 5 p.m. to 10 p.m. Use the graph to answer the questions which follow.

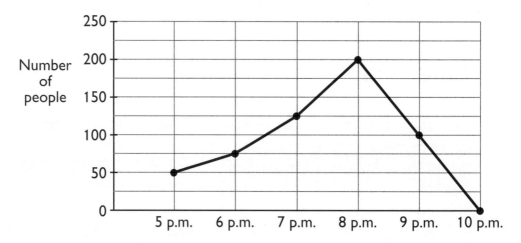

(a) What was the increase in the number of people from 7 p.m. to 8 p.m.?

(b) What was the decrease in the number of people from 8 p.m. to 9 p.m.?

2. The line graph shows the weekly sales of furniture made by a company during a 4-week trade fair. Use the graph to answer the questions which follow.

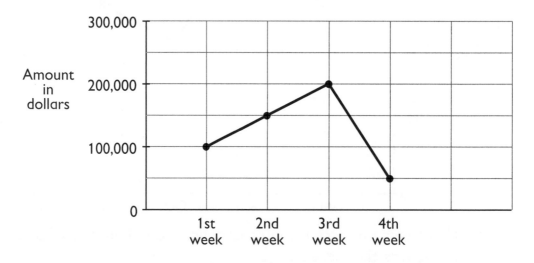

(a) The weekly sales decreased from $200,000 in the 3rd week to $50,000 in the 4th week. What was the decrease?

(b) What was the average weekly sales?

Workbook Exercise 36

3. This line graph shows the exchange rate between US dollars and Singapore dollars some years ago.

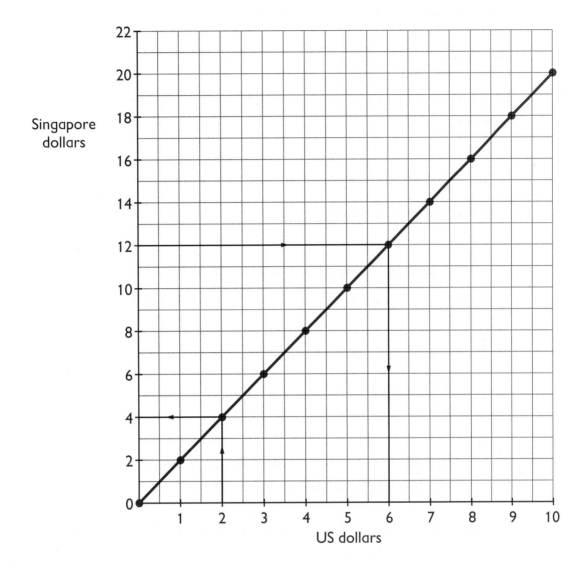

US$2 can be exchanged for Singapore $4.

Singapore $12 can be exchanged for US$6.

(a) How many Singapore dollars can be exchanged for US$9?
(b) How many US dollars can be exchanged for Singapore $10?
(c) How many US dollars can be exchanged for Singapore $16?

Workbook Exercise 37

REVIEW B

1. Find the value of each of the following:
   (a) $16 + 3 \times 8 \div 4$
   (b) $30 + 85 \times 2 \div (8 + 9)$
   (c) $(220 \div 11) \times (28 - 5)$
   (d) $12 + (30 - 14) \div 4 \times 5$

2. Multiply 2.56 by 32. Then round off the answer to the nearest whole number.

3. $\frac{2}{3}$ of a box of paper clips are red and the rest are green. If there are 120 red paper clips, how many green paper clips are there?

4. Mr. Reed packed $\frac{3}{4}$ kg of cookies equally into 3 bags. Find the weight of each bag of cookies. Give the answer in kilograms.

5. Mr. Lee's monthly salary is $2500. He gives $\frac{1}{5}$ of it to his wife and spends $\frac{3}{4}$ of the remainder. How much money does he spend each month?

6. The lengths of 3 rods are in the ratio 1 : 3 : 4. If the total length is 96 cm, find the length of the longest rod.

7. Carlos has $2.50. Tom has twice as much as Carlos. Ryan has $5 more than Tom. How much do the three boys have altogether?

8. After cutting off a length of 6.32 m from a rope 20 m long, the remainder is divided into 8 equal pieces. What is the length of each piece? Give the answer in meters.

9. What percentage of each figure is shaded?
   (a)
   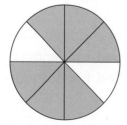
   (b)
   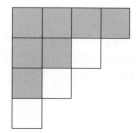

10. Express 80% as a decimal.

11. Express 36% as a fraction in its simplest form.

12. Express each of the following as a percentage.

    (a) 0.9   (b) 0.08   (c) $\dfrac{29}{50}$ (d) $\dfrac{27}{300}$

13. Find the value of each of the following:

    (a) 7% of 160   (b) 80% of 98 kg   (c) 15% of $21

14. 150 students took a Mathematics test. 98% of them passed the test. How many students passed the test?

15. Brandy made 250 donuts. She sold 90% of them. How many donuts did she have left?

16. Lynn deposits $5000 in a bank which pays 4% interest per year. How much money will she have in the bank after 1 year?

17. The usual price of a pair of shoes was $45. It was sold at a discount of 20%. Find the selling price.

18. A pool is filled with water at the rate of 20 liters per minute. How long will it take to fill the pool with 800 liters of water?

19. The table shows the postage rates for sending airmail packages to Japan.

For first 250 g	$20.00
For every additional 250 g	$2.80

Find the postage for sending a package which weighs 800 g.

20. Find the area of the shaded part of the rectangle.

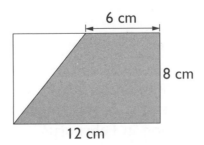

6 cm

8 cm

12 cm

21. Find the area of the shaded triangle.

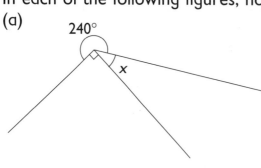

13 in.

8 in.

5 in.

4 in.

22. In each of the following figures, not drawn to scale, find ∠x.
(a)

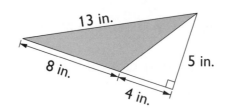

240°

x

(b) AOB and COD are straight lines.

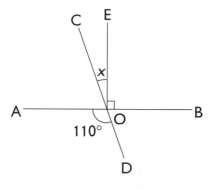

C E

x

A ——————— B

110°

O

D

23. The graph shows the amount of gas Jake bought in the last 6 months. Use the graph to answer the questions which follow.

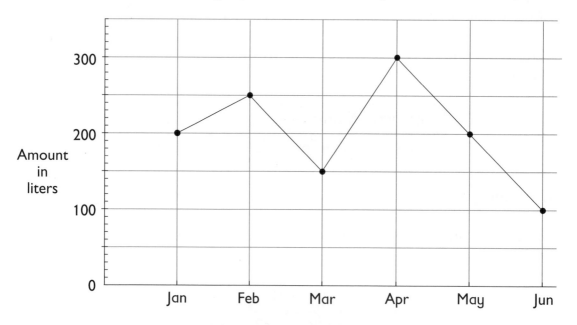

(a) Find the average amount of gas he bought each month.
(b) If 1 liter of gas cost $1.15, how much less money did he spend on gas in March than in February?

6 Triangles

1 Sum of Angles of a Triangle

Trace and cut out this triangle.

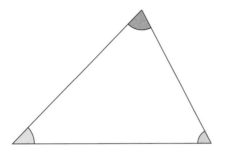

Then cut the triangle into 3 pieces as shown.

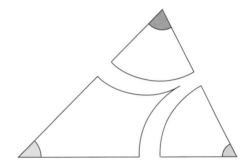

What do you notice when you arrange the 3 pieces like this?

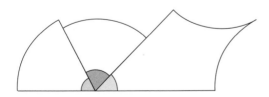

What is the sum of the three angles?

The three angles of a triangle add up to 180°.

1. Measure and add up the angles in each triangle.

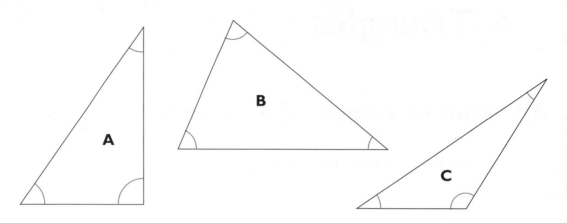

2. In triangle ABC, ∠ABC = 82° and ∠BAC = 54°. Find ∠BCA.

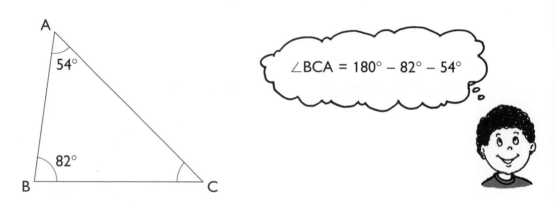

∠BCA = 180° − 82° − 54°

3. Find the unknown marked angle in each triangle.

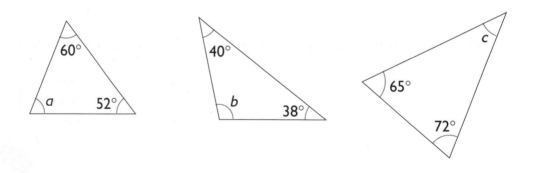

Workbook Exercise 38

4. Fold a right-angled triangle like this:

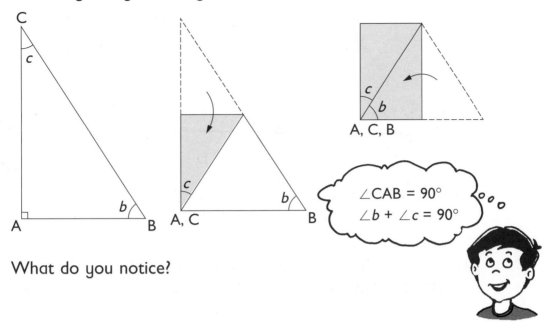

A, C, B

∠CAB = 90°
∠b + ∠c = 90°

What do you notice?

When one angle of a triangle is a right angle, the other two angles add up to **90°**.

5. In triangle PQR, ∠QPR is a right angle and ∠PQR = 57°.
Find ∠PRQ.

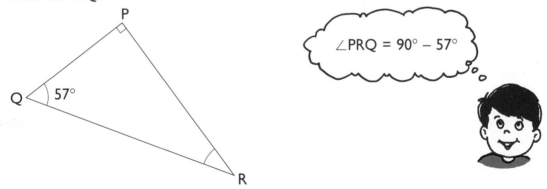

∠PRQ = 90° − 57°

6. Which of the following figures are right-angled triangles?

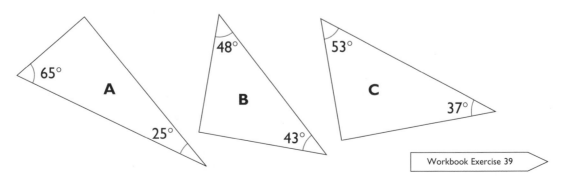

65°
A
25°

48°
B
43°

53°
C
37°

Workbook Exercise 39

7. In triangle ABC, BC is extended to D.

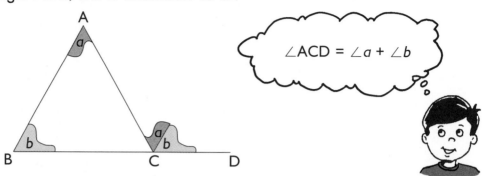

∠ACD is an exterior angle of the triangle.
∠a and ∠b are interior opposite angles of ∠ACD.

> The exterior angle of a triangle is equal to the sum of the interior opposite angles.

8. In triangle XYZ, YZ is extended to P, ∠ZXY = 50° and ∠XYZ = 34°. Find ∠XZP.

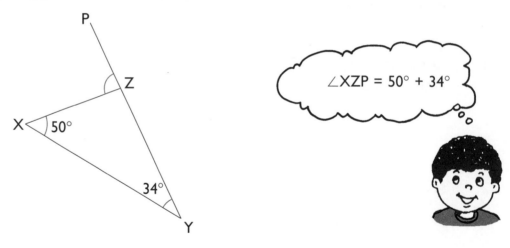

9. In each figure, ACD is a straight line. Find the unknown marked angle.

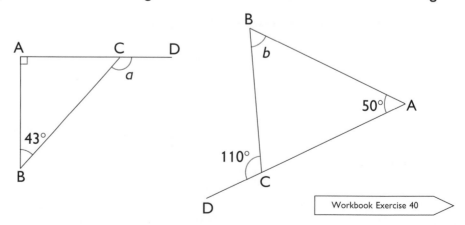

Workbook Exercise 40

Isosceles and Equilateral Triangles

Courtney used straws of different lengths to make these triangles.

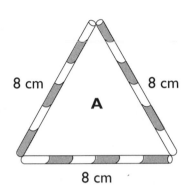

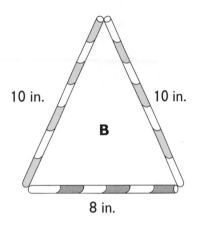

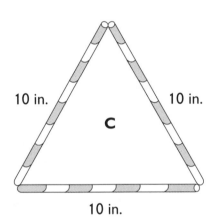

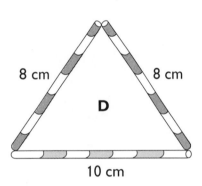

Which triangles have two equal sides?
What are they called?

Which triangles have three equal sides?
What are they called?

1. Fold an isosceles triangle in half as shown. What do you notice?

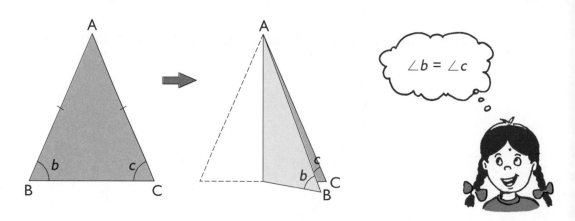

The angles opposite the equal sides are equal.

2. In triangle XYZ, ∠YXZ = ∠YZX. Is the triangle an isosceles triangle?

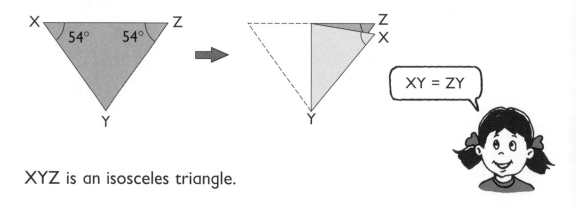

XYZ is an isosceles triangle.

3. Which of the following are isosceles triangles?

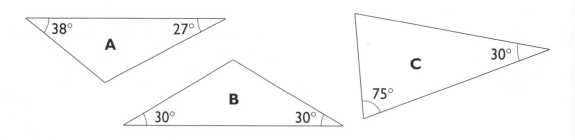

Workbook Exercise 41

4.

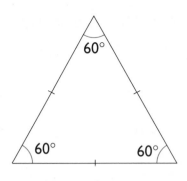

An equilateral triangle has 3 equal sides and 3 equal angles.
Each angle is 60°.

Which of the following are equilateral triangles?

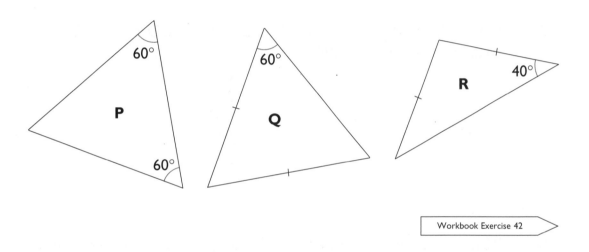

Workbook Exercise 42

5.   In triangle ABC, AB = AC and $\angle$ABC = 35°. Find $\angle$ACB and $\angle$BAC.

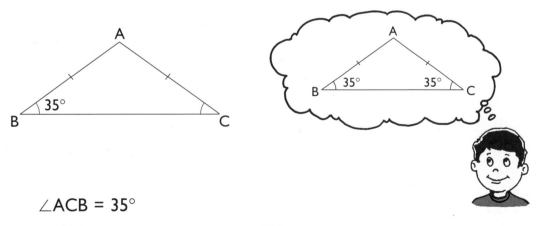

$\angle$ACB = 35°

$\angle$BAC = 180° − 35° − 35° = ■°

6. In triangle PQR, QR = PR and ∠PQR = 65°. QRS is a straight line. Find ∠PRS.

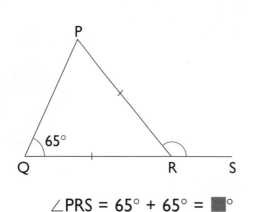 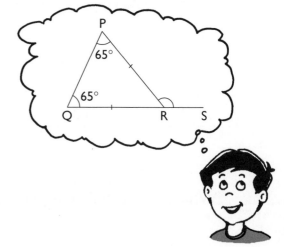

∠PRS = 65° + 65° = ▮°

7. In the figure, AB = AC and ∠DCE = 75°. BCD and ACE are straight lines. Find ∠ABC.

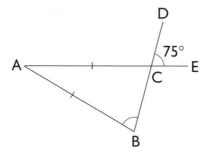

8. BCD is a straight line in each figure. Find the unknown marked angle.

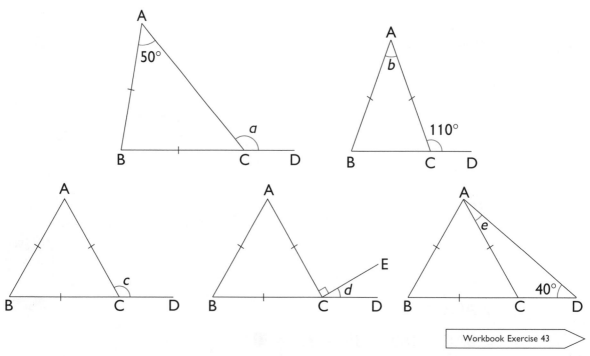

Workbook Exercise 43

③ Drawing Triangles

Ali uses straws to make a triangle like this:

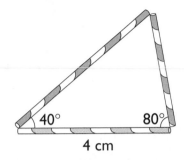

Then he draws the triangle.

First, I draw the side 4 cm long. Then, I draw the two angles using a protractor.

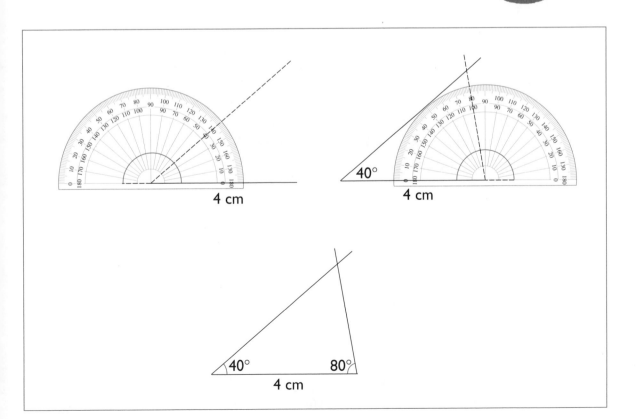

1. Draw a triangle PQR in which PQ = 5 cm, ∠PQR = 90° and ∠QPR = 40°.

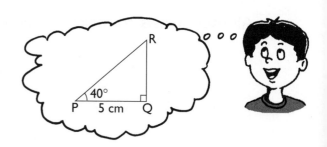

Step 1: Draw PQ = 5 cm.
Draw a line perpendicular to PQ through Q.

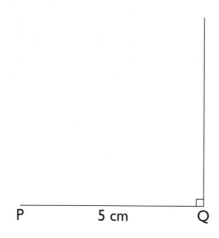

Step 2: Use a protractor to draw an angle of size 40° at P to locate the point R.

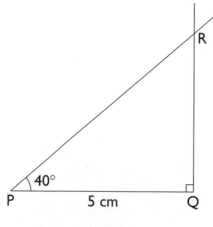

2. Draw a triangle ABC in which AB = 6 cm, BC = 4 cm and ∠ABC = 60°.

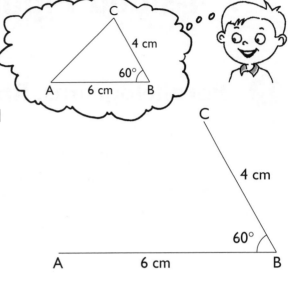

Step 1: Draw AB = 6 cm.
Draw ∠ABC = 60° and
BC = 4 cm.

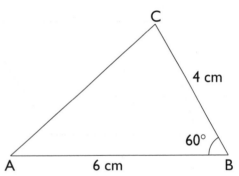

Step 2: Join AC.

3. Draw each of the following triangles with the given measurements.

(a)

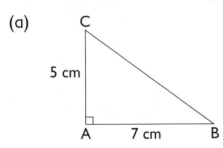

(b)

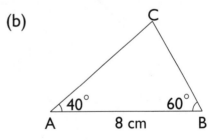

(c)

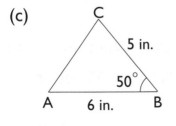

(d)

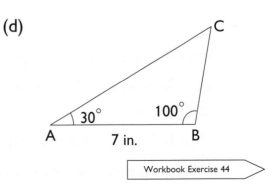

Workbook Exercise 44

67

7 4-sided Figures

1 Parallelograms, Rhombuses and Trapezoids

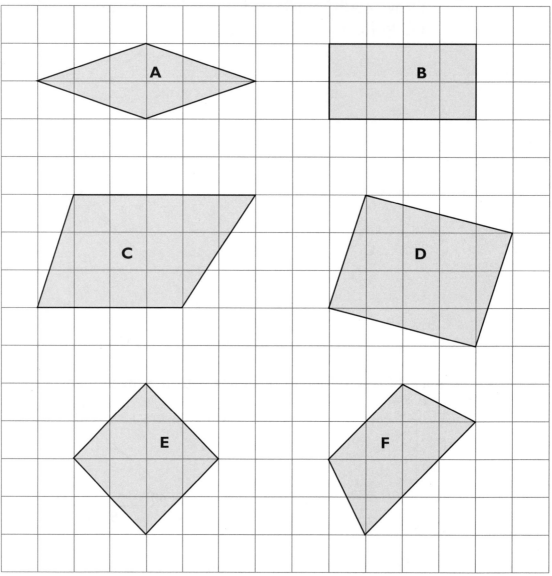

Which figures have two pairs of parallel lines? What are they called?

Which figures have only one pair of parallel lines? What are they called?

Which figures have four equal sides? What are they called?

Which figures have four right angles? What are they called?

1. Trace and cut out this parallelogram.

Then cut the parallelogram into two pieces and match the angles as shown.

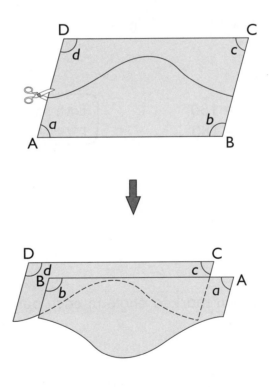

$\angle a = \angle c$
$\angle b = \angle d$

The opposite angles of a parallelogram are equal.

2. (a)

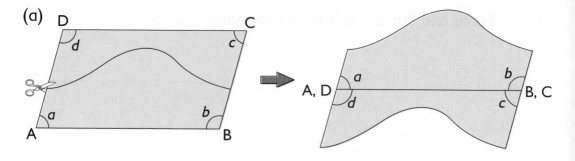

$$\angle a + \angle d = 180°$$
$$\angle b + \angle c = 180°$$

(b)

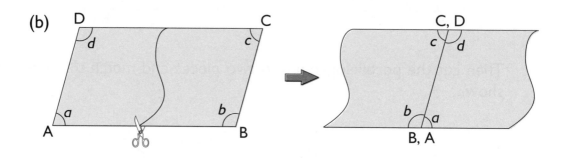

$$\angle a + \angle b = 180°$$
$$\angle c + \angle d = 180°$$

Each pair of angles between two parallel sides add up to 180°.

3. Find the unknown marked angle in each parallelogram.

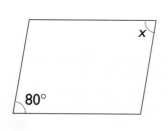

80°

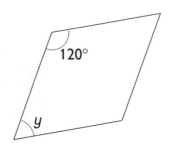

120°

y

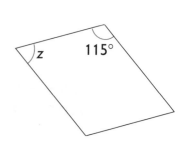

z   115°

Workbook Exercise 45

4.   Find the unknown marked angle in each rhombus.

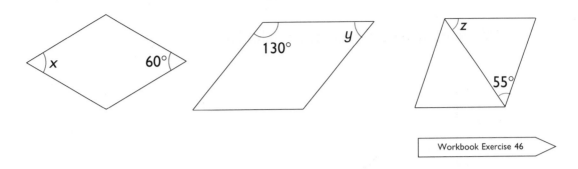

Workbook Exercise 46

5.   In trapezoid ABCD, AD//BC. Find ∠ABC and ∠DCB.

∠ABC = 180° − 50°

     = ■°

∠DCB = 180° − 120°

     = ■°

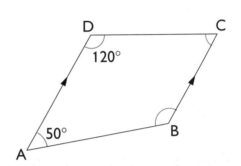

Each pair of angles between two parallel sides add up to 180°.

6.   Find the unknown marked angle in each trapezoid.

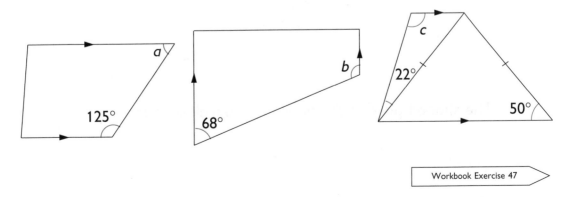

Workbook Exercise 47

② Drawing Parallelograms and Rhombuses

Weiming draws a pair of parallel lines.

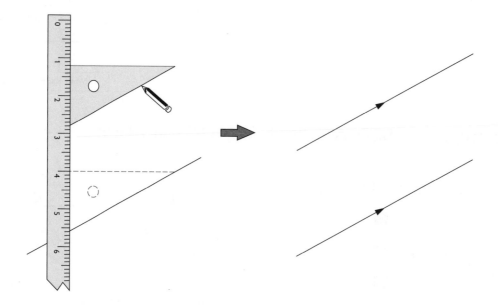

Then he draws another pair of parallel lines.

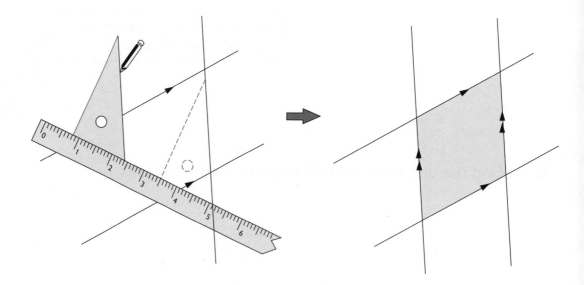

The shaded part of the figure is a parallelogram.

1.   Draw a rectangle ABCD in which AB = 6 cm and AD = 3 cm.

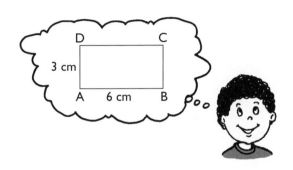

Step 1:   Draw AB = 6 cm.
Draw DA ⊥ AB
and DA = 3 cm.
Draw CB ⊥ AB
and CB = 3 cm.

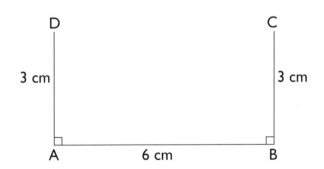

Step 2:   Join DC.

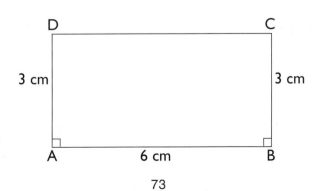

2. Draw a parallelogram ABCD in which AB = 4 cm, AD = 3 cm and ∠DAB = 60°.

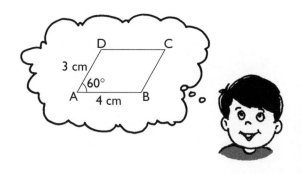

Step 1: Draw AB = 4 cm.
Draw ∠DAB = 60°
and AD = 3 cm.

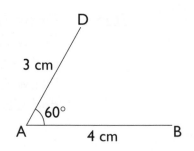

Step 2: Draw BC//AD
and BC = 3 cm.

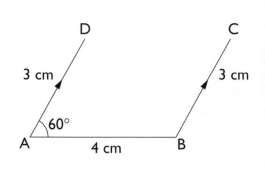

Step 3: Join DC.

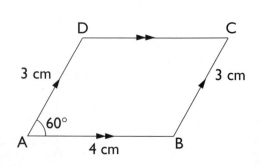

3. Draw parallelogram PQRS with the
    given measurements.

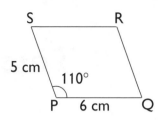

4. Draw a rhombus ABCD in which AB = 4 cm and ∠DAB = 40°.

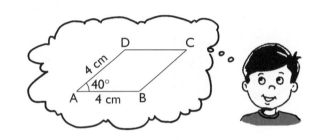

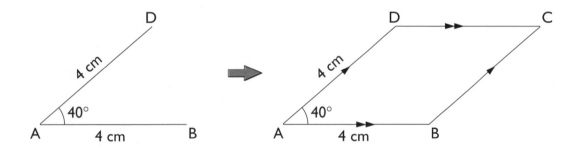

5. Draw rhombus ABCD with the given
    measurements.

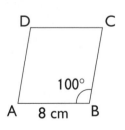

Workbook Exercise 48

8 Tessellations

1 Tiling Patterns

These tiling patterns are **tessellations**.
Each of them is made with one shape only.

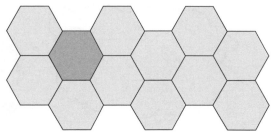

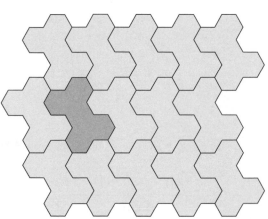

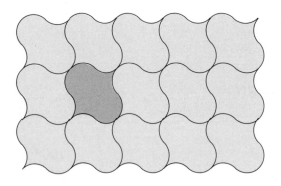

In a tessellation, the tiles
are fitted together with
no gaps in between.

Look for some tessellations around you.

1. What shape is used in each of the following tessellations?

(a)

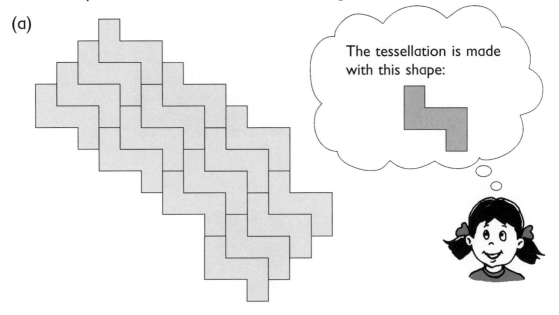

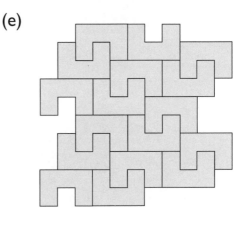

The tessellation is made with this shape:

(b)

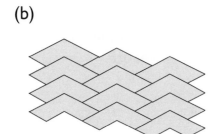

(c)

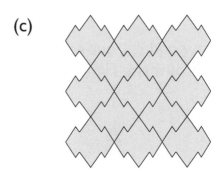

(d)

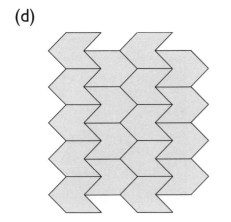

(e)

Workbook Exercise 49

2. A rectangle can tessellate.

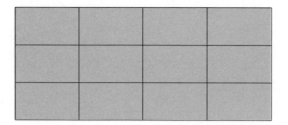

A circle cannot tessellate.

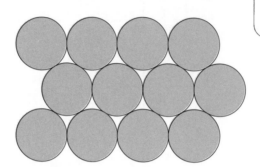

There are gaps in between the circles.

Draw and cut out each of the following shapes. Make 12 copies of each of them. Find out which shapes can tessellate.

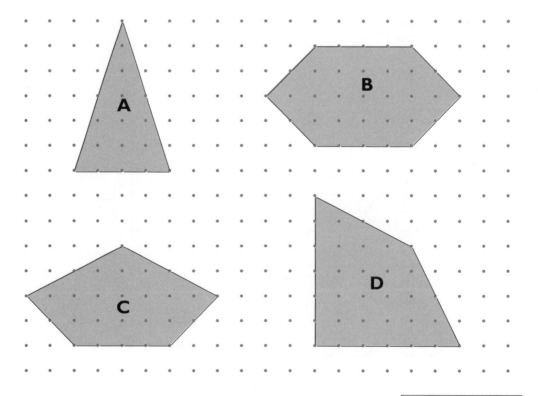

Workbook Exercise 50

3. Draw and cut out many copies of this rectangle.

Use them to make these two tessellations.

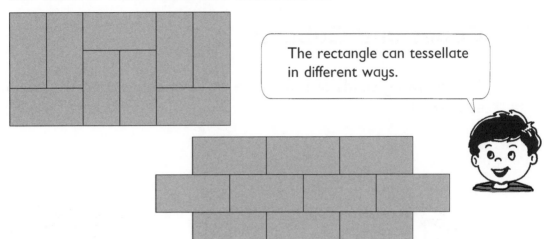

The rectangle can tessellate in different ways.

Make other tessellations with the rectangle.

4. Make as many different tessellations as you can using each of the following shapes.

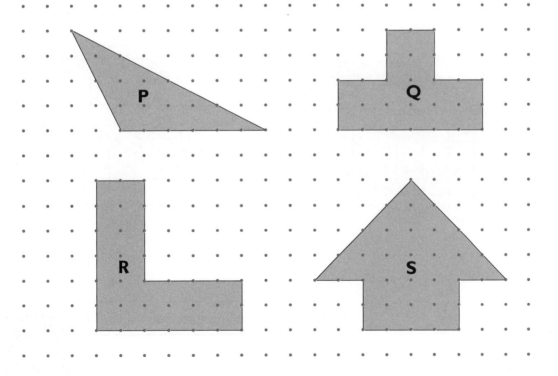

Workbook Exercises 51 & 52

9 Volume

1 Cubes and Cuboids

The following solids are made up of 1-cm cubes. Find the volume of each solid.

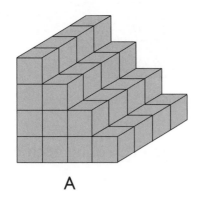

A

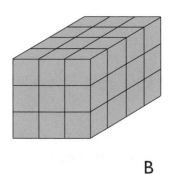

B

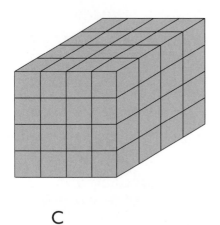

C

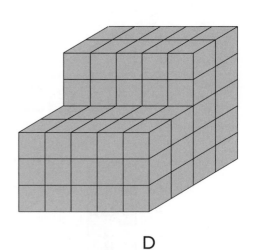

D

Which solid has the greatest volume?

1. The volume of a cube is 27 cm³. Find the length of one edge of the cube.

$$\blacksquare \times \blacksquare \times \blacksquare = 27$$

The length of one edge of the cube is $\blacksquare$ cm.

2. The volume of a cuboid is 24 cm³. The length of the cuboid is 3 cm and its width is 2 cm. Find its height.

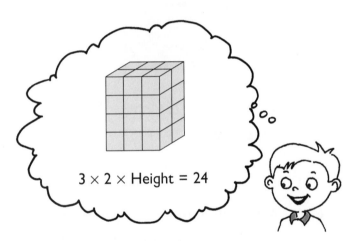

$3 \times 2 \times \text{Height} = 24$

$$\text{Height} = \frac{24}{3 \times 2}$$
$$= \blacksquare \text{ cm}$$

3. Find the unknown edge of each cuboid.

(a)

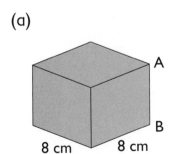

8 cm   8 cm

Volume = 576 cm³

AB = $\blacksquare$ cm

(b)

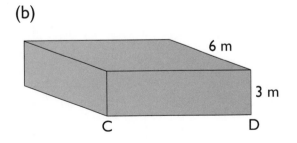

6 m

3 m

Volume = 216 m³

CD = $\blacksquare$ m

81

4. A rectangular container, 20 cm long and 10 cm wide, contains 2.5 liters of water. Find the height of the water level in the container. (1 ℓ = 1000 cm³)

Volume of water = 2.5 ℓ

= 2.5 × 1000 cm³

= 2500 cm³

Height of water level = $\dfrac{2500}{20 \times 10}$

= ■ cm

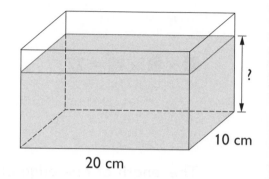

?

10 cm

20 cm

5. Find the unknown edge of each cuboid.

(a)

Area = 66 cm²

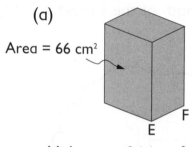

F

E

Volume = 264 cm³

EF = ■ cm

(b) Area = 72ft²

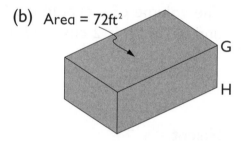

G

H

Volume = 288 ft³

GH = ■ ft

Workbook Exercise 53

6. A rectangular container measuring 20 cm by 10 cm by 10 cm is filled with water to its brim. If 750 cm³ of water is poured out from the container, what will be the height of the water level?

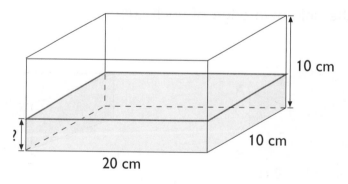

10 cm

10 cm

?

20 cm

Decrease in height of water level = $\dfrac{750}{20 \times 10}$ = ■ cm

Height of water level = ■ cm

Workbook Exercise 54

② Finding the Volume of a Solid

Samy poured 50 ml of water into a measuring cylinder. Then he put in some marbles and measured the volume of water displaced by the marbles.

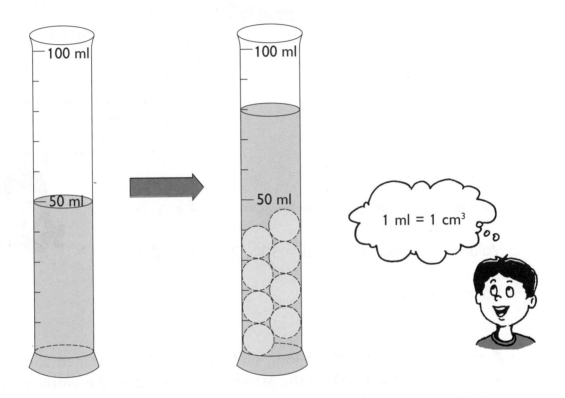

Volume of water = 50 cm³

Volume of water and the marbles = ■ cm³

Volume of the marbles = ■ cm³

Volume of marbles = Volume of water displaced

1. A rectangular tank, 30 cm long and 20 cm wide, is filled with water to a depth of 8 cm. When a stone was put in, the water level rose to 11 cm. Find the volume of the stone. (Assume that the stone is completely under water.)

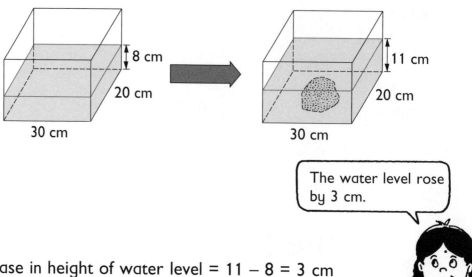

The water level rose by 3 cm.

Increase in height of water level = 11 − 8 = 3 cm

Volume of water displaced = 30 × 20 × 3 = ■ cm³

Volume of stone = ■ cm³

2. A rectangular tank, 30 cm long and 18 cm wide, contained some water and a stone. When the stone was taken out, the water level dropped by 2 cm. Find the volume of the stone. (Assume that the stone was completely under water.)

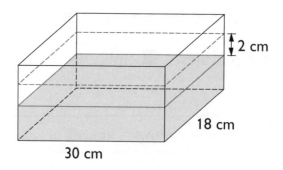

Decrease in height of water level = 2 cm

Volume of stone = 30 × 18 × 2 = ■ cm³

Workbook Exercise 55

PRACTICE 9A

1. Find the unknown edge of each cuboid.

    (a)

    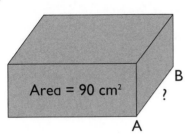

    Volume = 360 cm³

    AB = ■ cm

    (b)

    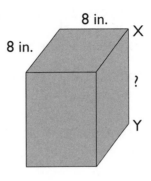

    Volume = 576 in.³

    XY = ■ in.

2. The volume of a cube is 125 in.³. Find the length of each edge of the cube.

    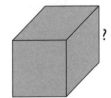

3. A rectangular container contains 1.2 liters of water. The area of the base of the tank is 96 cm². Find the height of the water level. (1 ℓ = 1000 cm³)

    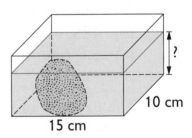

4. A rectangular container, 15 cm long and 10 cm wide, contains water to a depth of 4 cm. When a stone of volume 300 cm³ is put in, the water level rises. Find the height of the new water level. (Assume that the stone is completely under water.)

    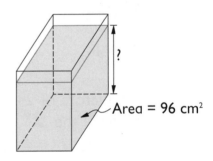

5. A rectangular container, 9 cm long and 6 cm wide, was filled with water to a depth of 5 cm. When some marbles were added into the container, the depth of the water became 7 cm. Find the total volume of the marbles.

    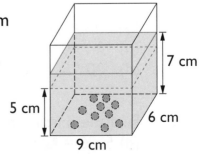

REVIEW C

1. (a) Express $2\frac{1}{4}$ kg in grams.

   (b) Express 3 km 90 m in kilometers.

   (c) Express $2\frac{3}{10}$ m in meters and centimeters.

2. A concert started at 7:15 p.m. and lasted $1\frac{2}{3}$ hours. At what time did it end?

3. $\frac{2}{5}$ of the people at a concert are children. $\frac{1}{4}$ of the children are boys. What fraction of the people at the concert are boys?

4. 1 kg of beef costs $12. Find the cost of $\frac{3}{4}$ kg of beef.

5. $\frac{5}{8}$ of a sum of money is $240. What is the value of the sum of money?

6. The factors of 24 are 1, 2, 3, 4, 6, 8, ■ and 24. What is the missing factor in the ■?

7. Find the average value of each of the following set of data.
   (a) 185,   103,   127,   165
   (b) 3.8 cm,   2.7 cm,   4.5 cm,   1.6 cm

8. The average of five numbers is 40. If four of the numbers are 18, 27, 37 and 50, what is the fifth number?

9. Express each ratio in its simplest form.
   (a) 2 : 10   (b) 6 : 12   (c) 21 : 14
   (d) 20 : 5   (e) 40 : 16   (f) 4 : 100

10. Find the missing number in each ■.
    (a) 5 : 6 = ■ : 18   (b) 30 : 48 = 5 : ■

11. $\frac{2}{5}$ of the 40 students in a class are girls. $\frac{1}{4}$ of the girls wear glasses. How many girls do not wear glasses?

12. Jason had 14 boxes of apples for sale. There were 36 apples in each box. He sold $\frac{5}{6}$ of the apples and threw away $\frac{1}{6}$ of the remainder which were rotten. How many apples did he have left?

13. After spending $\frac{2}{5}$ of her money on a handbag and $20 on a belt, Mary had $25 left. How much money did she have at first?

14. $\frac{3}{5}$ of a group of children are boys. There are 12 more boys than girls. How many girls are there?

15. The ratio of the number of red buttons to the number of green buttons is 4 : 3. There are 20 red buttons.
    (a) How many green buttons are there?
    (b) How many buttons are there altogether?

16. Lily, Carla and Gwen shared $156 in the ratio 3 : 2 : 7.
    (a) How much money did Carla receive?
    (b) How much more money did Gwen receive than Lily?

17. Mrs. Washington made 500 cookies. She sold 96% of them. How many cookies did she sell?

18. Marisol had $350. She spent 35% of the money on a pressure cooker. How much money did she have left?

19. The usual price of a motorcycle was $3600. Eric bought the motorcycle at a discount of 15%. How much did he pay?

20. The cost of a TV set was $640. Patrick sold it at 10% above the cost price. Find the selling price.

21. The perimeter of a square is 36 cm. Find the area of the square.

22. A rectangular room is 6 m long and 5 m wide. $\frac{2}{3}$ of the floor of the room is carpeted. What area of the floor is carpeted?

23. A photograph measuring 28 cm by 25 cm is mounted on a rectangular cardboard, leaving a margin of 5 cm all around. Find the area of the cardboard not covered by the photograph.

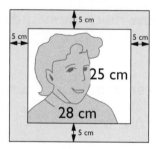

24. In the figure, ACE and BCD are straight lines. The figure is not drawn to scale. Find $\angle x$.

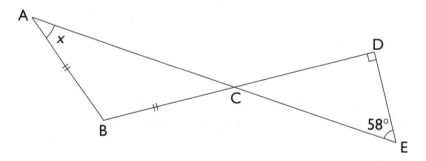

25. The area of the shaded face of the cuboid is 400 cm². Find the volume of the cuboid.

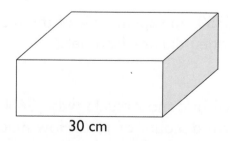

30 cm

26. Container A is filled with water to its brim. Container B is empty. If all the water in Container A is poured into Container B, what will be the height of the water level in Container B?

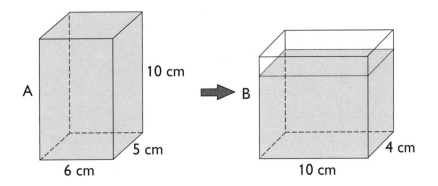

27. The average weight of 3 packages is 2.2 kg. The average weight of two of them is 1.8 kg. Find the weight of the third package.

28. An empty rectangular tank measures 50 cm by 30 cm by 20 cm. It is to be filled with water from a tap.
    (a) How many liters of water are needed to fill up the tank?
    (b) If water flows from the tap at the rate of 12 liters per minute, how long will it take to fill up the tank?
    (1 liter = 1000 cm^3)

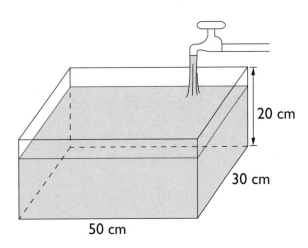

REVIEW D

1. Find the value of each of the following:
   (a) $60 \div (14 - 4) \times 3$ (b) $50 - 8 \times 2 + 16 \div 8$

2. Find the value of each of the following:
   (a) $4 - 1\frac{2}{3}$ (b) $72 \times \frac{7}{8}$

   (c) $\frac{3}{10} \times \frac{5}{6}$ (d) $\frac{8}{9} \div 6$

3. Write each of the following as a decimal.
   (a) $\frac{9}{100} + 3 + \frac{7}{10}$ (b) $\frac{37}{1000} + \frac{13}{100} + \frac{7}{10}$

4. Express 2.045 as a mixed number in its simplest form.

5. (a) Round off 3.952 to 1 decimal place.
   (b) Round off 7.639 to 2 decimal places.

6. An airplane traveled a distance of 2946 km. Round off the distance to the nearest 1000 km.

7. The average of 63, 74, ■ and 85 is 82. What is the missing number in the ■?

8. Express 20 : 12 : 56 in its simplest form.

9. (a) Express 20 out of 25 as a percentage.
   (b) Express 90 out of 200 as a percentage.

10. Express 48% as a fraction in its simplest form.

11. How many minutes are there in $2\frac{3}{5}$ hours?

12. A cake weighs 1.5 kg. Find the weight of $\frac{1}{2}$ of the cake.

13. Kate bought 8 spoons and 5 plates for $16.40. Each plate cost $1.20 more than each spoon. How much does each spoon cost?

14. A farmer sold 200 chickens at $3.50 each. With the money he received from the sale, he bought 30 turkeys. Find the cost of 1 turkey correct to the nearest cent.

15. The average weight of two boys is 48 kg. If one boy is 6 kg heavier than the other, find the weight of the heavier boy.

16. Sean spent $\frac{3}{5}$ of his money on a present for his mother. He spent $\frac{3}{4}$ of the remainder on a present for his sister.
    (a) What fraction of his money did he spend on the present for his sister?
    (b) If he spent $450 altogether, how much money did he have left?

17. A typist can type at a rate of 50 words per minute. How long will the typist take to type 4 pages each containing 300 words?

18. The rates of charges for taxi fare in a city are as follows:

For the first 1.5 km	$2.40
For every additional 100 m	$0.10

Find the taxi fare for a journey of 4 km.

19. The ratio of the number of men to the number of women in a club is 5 : 7. There are 12 more women than men. How many members are there altogether?

20. There are 1800 students in a school. 60% of them are boys. How many more boys than girls are there?

21. In each of the following figures, not drawn to scale, find $\angle y$.
    (a) BCD is a straight line.   (b) ABC and CDE are straight lines.

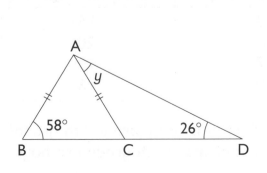

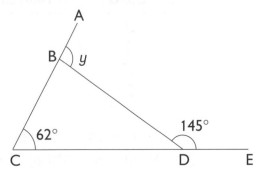

22. The figure is made up of a square and a triangle. The area of the square is 64 cm². Find the area of the triangle.

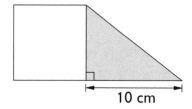

10 cm

23. A rectangular container, 40 cm long and 25 cm wide, is filled with 12 liters of water. Find the height of the water level in the container. (1 liter = 1000 cm³)

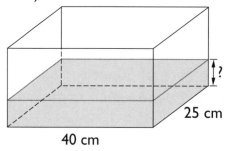

?

25 cm

40 cm

24. A rectangular container measuring 60 cm by 20 cm by 30 cm is filled with 28 liters of water. How many more liters of water are needed to fill the container to the brim? (1 liter = 1000 cm³)

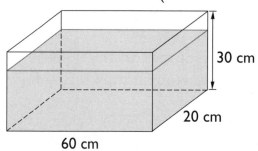

30 cm

20 cm

60 cm

25. A school has four classes in 5th grade. The table shows the number of boys and girls in each class.

Class	Number of boys	Number of girls
A	23	15
B	18	20
C	17	19
D	20	18

(a) How many more boys than girls are there in 5th grade?
(b) What percentage of the students in 5th grade are boys?

26. Use the given shape to make two different tessellations in the spaces provided.

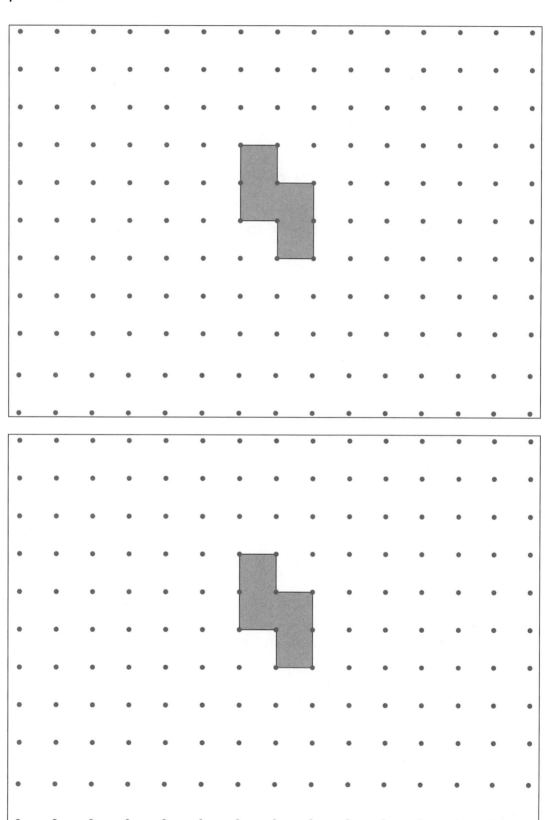

REVIEW E

1. Mr. Karlson bought 6576 lb of rice. He packed the rice in bags of 12 lb each.
   How many bags of rice did he have?

2. Jessica bought $\frac{3}{4}$ lb of berries.

   Mary bought $\frac{1}{6}$ lb of berries less than Jessica.

   (a) Find the weight in pounds of the berries Mary bought.
   (b) Find the total weight in pounds of the berries they bought.

3. Max has $\frac{4}{5}$ qt of apple juice. He drinks $\frac{1}{2}$ qt of it.

   How much apple juice does he have left?
   (Give the answer in quarts.)

4. A piece of wood is 5 ft long.
   Juan used $\frac{3}{4}$ of its length to make a shelf.

   What is the length in feet of the wood left?

5. Mrs. Meyer jogs $\frac{3}{4}$ mi a day.

   How many miles does she jog in 8 days?

6. Eric poured 10 gal of water into an empty tank.

   If $\frac{5}{6}$ of the tank was filled, find the capacity of the tank in gallons.

7. The area of a rectangle is 56 in.^{2}.
   If the width of a rectangle is 7 in., find its perimeter.

8. Arrange the numbers in increasing order.

    (a) $\frac{3}{4}$ lb, 11 oz, $\frac{13}{16}$ lb

    (b) 16 qt, 1.5 gal, 10 qt

    (c) 39 in., $1\frac{2}{3}$ yd, $3\frac{1}{6}$ ft

9. Make a table to show the following data:

Ryan	Alex	Jeff
Height: 21.5 in.	Height: 19 in.	Height: 20.5 in.
Weight: 7 lb 3 oz	Weight: 6 lb 2 oz	Weight: 6 lb 12 oz

10. Ten pieces of string, each 11 in. long, are cut from a length of string 253 in. long.
    What is the length in inches of the remaining piece of string?

11. Round off 245.675 ft to 2 decimal places.

12. A watermelon weighs 4 lb 5 oz. A pineapple weighs 1 lb 12 oz.
    How much heavier is the watermelon than the pineapple?
    (Give the answer in pounds and ounces.)

13. Multiply and divide in compound units.
    (a) 2 yd 2 ft × 5 = ■ yd ■ ft
    (b) 6 gal 3 qt × 6 = ■ gal ■ qt
    (c) 5 qt 2 c × 7 = ■ qt ■ c
    (d) 6 qt 1 pt × 4 = ■ qt ■ pt
    (e) 5 lb 12 oz ÷ 4 = ■ lb ■ oz
    (f) 3 ft 8 in. ÷ 11 = ■ ft ■ in.
    (g) 7 gal 2 qt ÷ 6 = ■ gal ■ qt

14. Find 3 ft 7 in. divided by 4 to the nearest inch.

15. Find the area of each triangle.

(a)

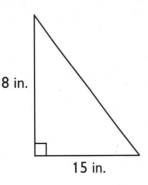
8 in.
15 in.

(b)

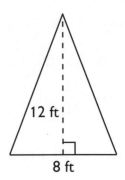
12 ft
8 ft

16. Find the volume of each cuboid.

(a)

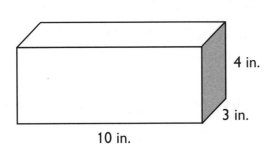
4 in.
3 in.
10 in.

(b)

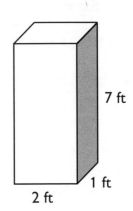
7 ft
2 ft
1 ft

17. The volume of a tank is 1080 in.^{3}.
If the base has an area of 72 in.^{2}, find its height.

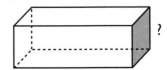
?

18. A fish tank is $\frac{2}{5}$ full after Sara poured 14 gal of water into it.

What is the full capacity of the tank in gallons?

19.   (a)   5 gal 3 qt = ◼ qt
      (b)   4 ft and 11 in. = ◼ in.
      (c)   5 lb 13 oz = ◼ oz
      (d)   3 qt 2 pt = ◼ pt

20.   (a)   15 c = ◼ qt ◼ c
      (b)   45 pt = ◼ qt ◼ pt
      (c)   52 gal = ◼ gal ◼ qt
      (d)   38 in. = ◼ ft ◼ in.